Capricorn

1996

TERI KING'S
ASTROLOGICAL HOROSCOPES
FOR 1996

Capricorn

Teri King's complete horoscope
for all those whose birthdays
fall between
22 December and 20 January

ELEMENT
Shaftesbury, Dorset ● Rockport, Massachusetts
Brisbane, Queensland

© Teri King 1995

First published in Great Britain in 1995 by
Element Books Limited
Shaftesbury, Dorset SP7 8BP

Published in the USA in 1995 by
Element, Inc.
42 Broadway, Rockport, MA 01966

Published in Australia in 1995 by
Element Books Limited
for Jacaranda Wiley Limited
33 Park Road, Milton, Brisbane 4064

Cover design by Max Fairbrother
Design by Roger Lightfoot
Typeset by Light Technology Ltd. Fife, Scotland
Printed and bound in Great Britain by
BPC Paperbacks Ltd., Aylesbury, Bucks

British Library Cataloguing in Publication
data available

Library of Congress Cataloging in Publication
data available

ISBN 1-85230-679-3

Element Books regrets that it cannot enter into any
correspondence with readers requesting information
about their horoscopes.

Contents

Introduction

Astrology has many uses, not least of these its ability help us to understand both ourselves and other people. Unfortunately there are many misconceptions and confusions associated with it, such as that old chestnut – how can the zodiac forecast be accurate for all millions of people born under one particular sign?

The answer to this is that all horoscopes published in newspapers, books and magazines are, of necessity a general nature. Unless an astrologer can work from the date, time and place of your birth, the reading given will only be true for the typical member of your sign.

For instance, let's take a person born on 9 August. This person is principally a subject of Leo, simply because the Sun occupied that section of the heavens known as Leo during 24 July to 23 August. However, when delving into astrology at its most serious, there are other influences which need to be taken into consideration, for example, the Moon. This planet enters a fresh sign every 48 hours. On the birth date in question it may have been in, say, Virgo. And if this were the case it would make our particular subject Leo (Sun representing willpower) and Virgo (Moon representing instincts) or if you will a Leo/Virgo. Then again the rising sign or 'ascendant' must also be taken into consideration. This also changes constantly as the earth revolves: approximately every two hours a new section of the heavens comes into view – a new sign passes over the horizon. The rising sign is of the utmost importance, determining the image projected by the subject to the outside world – in effect, the personality.

The time of birth is essential when compiling a birth chart. Let us suppose that in this particular instance Leo was rising at the time of birth. Now, because two of the three main influences are Leo, our sample case would be fairly typical of his/her sign, possessing all the faults and attributes associated with it. However, if on the other hand, the Moon and ascendant had been in Virgo then, whilst our subject would certainly display some of the Leo attributes or faults, it is more than likely that for the most part he/she would feel and behave more like a Virgoan.

As if life weren't complicated enough, this procedure must be carried through to take into account all the remaining planets. The position and signs of Mercury, Venus, Mars, Jupiter, Saturn, Uranus, Neptune and Pluto must all be discovered, plus the aspect formed from one planet to another. The calculation and interpretation of these movements by an astrologer will then produce an individual birth chart.

Because the heavens are constantly changing, people with identical charts are a very rare occurrence. Although it is not inconceivable that it could happen, this would mean that the two subjects were born not only on the same date and at the same time, but also in the same place. Should such an incident occur, then the deciding factors as to how these individuals would differ in their approach to life, love, career, financial prospects and so on would be due to environmental and parental influence.

Returning to our hypothetical Leo: our example with the rising Sun in Leo and Moon in Virgo, may find it useful not only to read up on his or her Sun sign (Leo) but also to read the section dealing with Virgo (the Moon). Nevertheless, this does not invalidate Sun sign astrology. This is because of the great power the Sun possesses, and on any chart this planet plays an important role.

Belief in astrology does not necessarily mean believing in totally determined lives, that we are predestined and have no control over our fate. But what it does clearly show is that our lives run in cycles, for both good and bad and, with the aid of astrology, we can make the most of, or minimize, certain patterns and tendencies. How this is done is entirely up to the individual. For example, if you are in possession of the knowledge that you are about to experience a lucky few days or weeks, then you can make the most of them by pushing ahead with plans. You can also be better prepared for illness, misfortune, romantic upset and every adversity.

Astrology should be used as it was originally intended – as as a guide, especially to character. In this direction it is invaluable and it can help us in all aspects of friendship, work and romance. It makes it easier for us to see ourselves as we really are and, what's more, as others see us. We can recognize both our own weaknesses and strengths and those of others. It can give us both outer confidence, and inner peace.

In the following pages you will find: personality profiles; an in-depth look at the year ahead from all possible angles including numerology; a look at the Uranus Life Cycle; monthly and daily guides; this year's Moon tables; plus, and it is a big plus, information for those poor and confused creatures so often ignored who are born on 'the cusp' – at the beginning or the end of each sign.

Used wisely, astrology can help you through life. It is not intended to encourage complacency, since in the final analysis what you do with your life is up to you. This book will aid you in adopting the correct attitude to the year ahead and thus maximizing your chances of success. Positive thinking is encouraged because this helps us to attract positive situations. Allow astrology to walk hand in hand with you and you will be increasing your chances of success and happiness.

A Fresh Look at Your Sun Sign

As a rule, members of the general public appreciate and understand that for practical reasons Sun sign astrology is fairly general, and therefore for a more in-depth study it is necessary to hire an astrologer who will then proceed to study the date, year, place and time of birth of an individual. Then, by correlating the birth chart with the positions of the different planets, a picture can slowly drawn for the client.

However, there is also a middle way, which can be illuminating. Each sign comprises 30 'degrees' (or days) and, by reducing these down into three sections becomes possible to draw up a picture of each sign which is far more intimate than the usual methods. Therefore, check out your date of birth and draw your own conculsions from the information below.

CAPRICORN (22 DECEMBER TO 20 JANUARY)

BORN BETWEEN 22 DECEMBER AND 1 JANUARY

Your Sun falls in the first section of Capricorn, making you ambitious, often solemn, successful and somewhat detached on occasions. You are also disciplined and hardworking and prone to depressive moods.

The ideas and opinions of other people tend to be of great importance to you. This is because you are basically insecure in yourself. Therefore you are inclined to socialize with those whom you respect since you see yourself reflected in your relationships. It is very much a case of 'who you know and not what you know' that counts with you.

You are inclined to be status conscious and critical, and you prefer that people don't take up your time unnecessarily. At the same time, you are dutiful, devoted and often loyal towards those people to whom you are deeply committed.

Because you have plenty of common sense and practical ability, plus an earthy personality, you have little time and patience with the flighty members of the human race who never seem to know whether they are coming or going. For the most part, you are drawn to people with qualities of strength, honesty, stability and intelligence and who have accomplished a great deal in this world. In other words, you have the highest personal ideals.

When it comes to your personal life, and especially where love is concerned, you are drawn to those who are in prominent positions. However, due to your deepseated insecurities, you frequently become involved with people beneath your own level of accomplishment as they tend to make you look good in the eyes of the world.

Because your own drive for status is so important, you ultimately dismiss from your life and your social circle those who you feel are in a position to bring you down. It is very likely that by the middle of your life you will have proved your own worth and are likely to have found success in a highly competitive society.

BORN BETWEEN 2 JANUARY AND 11 JANUARY

Your Sun falls in the second section of Capricorn, giving you a tremendous amount of charm and sociability. It is likely that you are gifted in a creative way. In business you are very shrewd where financial matters are concerned, and in your social life you show a gracious and unmistakable flair.

It is likely that you are a highly productive person who is driven to work a great deal and sleep very little. You are tactful, understanding, sincere, kind, adaptable and diplomatic. You possess a highly individualistic and unique value system which helps you when it comes to determining your life objectives. You climb towards these objectives with a bravery and a tenacity that are never deflected.

Capricorns born in this section have an overwhelming need to make concrete their desires, despite the strength of any opposition they are confronted with and they do it with such dogged determination that others, including rivals, look on with fascination.

Subjects of this section often show an inclination to subdue the pleasure principle should a situation of long-term profit be at stake. Furthermore they feel a sense of great dedication to professional duties and ideals as well as exhibiting a conscientious approach towards details.

On the romantic side, early in your life there is likely to have been some disappointment and heartache from a destroyed marriage or relationship. However, if you can fight an inclination to become embittered or disillusioned about this, then it is likely that this unfortunate experience will be followed by an extremely happy union with a devoted, loyal mate.

Capricorns born in this section possess a powerful and determined will. The moment you come to trust and rely on it is the time when your potential will become limitless.

BORN BETWEEN 12 JANUARY AND 20 JANUARY

Your Sun falls in the third section of Capricorn. Because of this, you are a Utopian whose ideals tend to become caught between logic and emotions. This frequently causes you to suffer extreme anxiety when confronted with choices that will significantly affect your life. You are inclined to brood about past mistakes and decisions and often bring on your own states of depression.

Certainly your mind can be highly disciplined when you refuse to allow it to control you through negative mood swings and depressions. You are an intellectual person with a steady nature and a strong sense of purpose and destiny.

Although you can become bogged down with details of an administrative nature, you frequently have your own interests, often in the sort of creative activities that could be put to professional use. However, first you must confront your own fears and phobias because they can severely restrict your potential for growth and expansion.

Because you are modest and shy, you often have problems, either of making yourself heard or of communicating on a deep level. Although your ideas can be viable and strong, your means of expressing them tend to be incoherent or weak, as a result of which you often suffer from a lack of publicity.

There is a latent writing ability and verbal talent in this section. However, first you must be able to trust yourself and believe that you are a powerful person. The world may very well be waiting for your talents and ideas. Consider the notion that you might be doing everyone around you a favour by pushing yourself into the limelight. Be more prepared to participate in the world around you. In this way you will be making the most of your potential.

WHEN YOU ARE BAD YOU ARE VERY VERY BAD (Horrorscopes)

There is a tendency for you to be condescending towards others due to a complex which compels you to try to control people. You tend to be shackled to your own will and you suffer nagging discontent if you do not feel free to enact your power play.

Because of your great ego problems, you experience a need always to be on top. One of your favourite experiences is ordering other people around and telling them what to do as if they were incompetents who can function without the 'pearls of wisdom' you subject them to.

You are patronizing, domineering and arrogant, and you tend to override the feelings of others to such a degree that you treat them as if they were pieces of furniture. You are inclined to judge other people by their success and to ingratiate yourself with them. You have precious little time or patience for those who are beneath you, and you deliberately cultivate the more successful members of the human race. Because of your self-obsession, you live each day in the hope that it will bring you closer to being able to exercise your power games.

Other people might call you stuffy, others again a sourpuss; this is because of your obvious self-importance and your surprising way of taking others down and trampling on their egos. Your motivating principle drives you to prove your superiority, and you need to demonstrate other people's inferiority.

Your personality is so infuriating that it could bring a saint to contemplate homocide. After a while of listening to you, others will do anything to keep you quiet. You are inclined to boast in an effort to convince the world that you are something that you really are not.

When it comes to love, you have a way of making the opposite sex feel as if you have just rescued them from a fate worse than death. One of the most interesting and complicated things about you is that when you have made up your mind that a certain person is your soulmate, then you proceed to disregard totally their thoughts and opinions.

Your fundamental attitude to your partner is that he or she was meant to live to serve you and should be sensitive enough to know when to keep quiet and listen to what you have to say. Their thoughts and opinions are completely ignored, since you believe that you always know best.

Because a mate is as necessary to you as a pair of shoes or a nice warm bed, it is important to ensure that you get the type that looks good but costs least. If after a certain amount of time has elapsed it begins to dawn on you that the person concerned just isn't interested, then you become morose, hostile and defensive. For in your mind it is only *your* feelings that matter, since he or she simply isn't allowed the right to have any opinions themselves. Despite this, you never give up and proceed to apply pressure until your victim's resistance fades away and they are left grovelling for peace. However, you are oblivious to their plight. To you, all that is important is power, the kind that will put you at the top where you can rule your kingdom with an iron fist.

CUSP CASES

CAPRICORN/SAGITTARIUS CUSP: 19–24 DECEMBER

When the heat of the furnace of Sagittarius is combined with the powerful dynamics associated with the earthy Capricorn, great leadership, achievement and success are all possible. This combination makes you generous, traditional, freedom-loving and restrained. Furthermore you are cautious, independent and inclined to produce a slight conflict between your inner and outer personality and needs.

Your natural friendliness is blended with good judgement and foresight, therefore you are the sort of person who can usually make your fantasies come true. You make a formidable partner or adversary and one who has the power to excel both creatively and romantically yet at the same time give solid support to those who count.

CAPRICORN/AQUARIUS CUSP: 18–23 JANUARY

You are an inventive and eccentric genius with a large streak of common sense. Invariably you have your eye firmly fixed on the future, although you are also ready to learn from the past. With your leadership and organizational ability, plus your humanitarian ideals, you could make a successful and highly popular politician.

Your Capricorn side could hold back your Aquarian inclination to race ahead without due thought, and it will have the patience to see you through the tough times in life.

You love working with other people for their own benefit, something which is generally much appreciated by your mate. You are witty and articulate with a talent to amuse, a trait which is certainly appreciated and admired by the opposite sex.

The Year Ahead: Overview

There are many reasons why 1996 should be a memorable year. Among them is the fact that in January Uranus will have finally finished its long journey through your sign. As a Capricorn, you generally like to live your life at a steady pace – no unpleasant surprises please! However, there is no doubt, this particular planet has brought unwanted change, stress and many complications which you could well have done without. Now, it is somebody else's turn, and you certainly have reason for celebrating.

Yet another reason for jubilance can be found in the form of lucky and expansive Jupiter who will be sailing through your sign for the entire year. This will bring opportunities to improve yourself in all areas and, of course, it is up to you to be alert enough, as well as being prepared enough to make the necessary adjustments and calculated risks in order to make the most of this time.

Your ruling planet, Saturn, continues to plod through the sign of Pisces until early April. So, if you have experienced problems with brothers, sisters or methods of transport and short journeys, then relax, because this state of affairs will come to an end when this planet of yours moves on into the sign of Aries. Naturally, it had to go somewhere, and there may be some added responsibility in connection with the family and property. But, with your fighting spirit and determination, this is only viewed as a challenge and one that you could easily win with a positive frame of mind.

If your life has been plagued by a certain amount of mystery, scandal or unusual sets of circumstances, then I am afraid this may continue for a while longer. But then again, we do need something to pit our wits against, and, for you, it comes in the form of Neptune; don't worry, next year it will have moved on into somebody else's sign. In the meantime, remember this has a positive side too, because Neptune can bring increased inspiration and romance, and, if you are at all creative, you will have ideas popping out of your head, particularly if you are born rather late in the Capricorn phase.

Now, there are certain lessons to be learned here. You are always, whether you are prepared to admit it or not, concerned with your status, work and reputation. However, this is a time to recognize that there are other things in life, as it is likely you have all the tools, experience and ability to succeed. And, ideally, during this year you will be turning your attention, though not completely, to affairs connected with the home, family, property and maybe even parents. Because, whether it is conscious or unconscious, these are the aspects of life which motivate you. Not only that, but these areas help you to satisfy your deepest needs of satisfaction and pleasure.

This is as good a time as any for deciding exactly what kind of Goat you are. You could be a high-flying, sure-footed mountain Goat who proceeds through life a step at a time or a modest, retiring, domesticated soul who seems to be content to be tethered to the same old stake years on end, because the thought of trying anything new scares you stiff. You are sure to fall into one category or other; it is up to you to decide which applies.

Being a Goat isn't easy, as your manner can present problems. You are a little too reserved or stiff with other people, cautious and sometimes even brisk. Those who consider reaching out to you on first meeting are often put off by your reserve, coolness and obvious lack of response. This is not your fault; it is a peculiarity of make-up in the Capricorn character. You just can't help building an impenetrable wall around yourself to protect your sensitivity, because, although you are strong and fearless in a worldly way, you are terrified of being hurt emotionally. Others rarely guess that under that superb self-control, there is a soft, gentle and basically anxious person. Luckily, with Jupiter in your sign, you will feel more confident than you have for some time and, because of this, perhaps more prepared to allow others to get closer to you.

Perhaps the most important astrological phenomenon occurring this year is that Pluto has finally moved into the humanitarian sign of Sagittarius. Now, in retrospect it is quite obvious that Pluto, in the solar sign of Scorpio, has not been kind either to the planet or man himself. Scorpio is associated with plagues, war, turbulence, downfall and crime. Who would have thought in 1983, when it entered this sign, that it would herald the end of the Cold War and the falling of the Berlin Wall, and that a new plague would develop and grow with such alarming proportions?

Luckily, this planet has now entered Sagittarius so we can look forward to a good few years when great and wonderful medical breakthroughs will be discovered. Slowly, it will become apparent that man has finally left his turbulent teen years, is now reaching adulthood and is no longer prepared to fight other people simply because of the colour of their skin, or because their religion happens to be different. Even the leaders of the world will need to accept the fact that for the most part they have been elected by the people and, because of this, it is about time they started to put them first. Yes, we are beginning a period of awakening of man's consciousness which can only improve the quality of life on this planet as well as providing a healing time for Mother Earth herself who has certainly been battered around for some time now.

Career Year

This section of the book brings us to a very important truth about the Goat's nature. Underneath, it is likely that you are self-centred and sometimes intent on achieving your selfish ends. Now, this is not as bad as it sounds, because every sign is a bit selfish; some quite powerfully, which is definitely not your style. The Goat's way is to be on the lookout for the easy path up, and then to move in smoothly and easily. In other words, to use the earth beneath your feet to best advantage. To be honest, you don't exactly like hard work unless there is something in it for you, then you are a formidable worker, the Trojan of the stars.

When you meet up with an obstacle in your path, you don't waste time on it as some of the other signs do; you simply pick a good vantage point and jump over it. If that obstacle happens to be a person, your indifference to their feelings or wishes often earns you the reputation of being unsympathetic and opportunist.

Responsibility is the essence of your character. You may run from it for years, especially in youth, until you discover a purpose worth devoting your tremendous energies to. Then you become enormously ambitious, but usually in a quiet way. If you are tied to the duties of a housewife, or even househusband, you will assert your ambitious urges through your loved one. You will never be content to sit back and take it easy for too long. You must always be climbing, trying to get above your current circumstances. Mind you, as a Goat, you frequently stick very much to the mountain you are used to. You rarely attempt to explore greener-looking pastures because you have the wisdom to realize that they may look greener than your own, but this is simply an illusion. No, you prefer to stride to the summit of your own ambition with any means that happen to be at your disposal.

It has to be said that not only are you good at giving orders, you are also great at carrying them out, since you don't mind being told what to do. You make a conscientious and loyal helper. You are not hampered by ego. You see nothing wrong in serving other people faithfully; partly, this is because of your firm belief that no matter where you begin you will gradually rise to a position of security or power, even both. In many ways you are like your fellow earth sign, Virgo, built to serve with reliability, but you possess the added advantage of being able to reach the top of executive power and authority. Your resourcefulness, resolution and enterprise, along with your tremendous ability to plan, fits you for organizational and commercial empire-building. It is not rare for Capricorn captains of industry to have started off in the humblest of jobs or from the most deprived backgrounds. All this means to you is that you have a little further to travel in order to achieve those ambitions of yours.

Now, let's have a look at the year ahead from the professional viewpoint. Well, with Jupiter in your sign for the entire period, you have that extra touch of magic about you, if you are involved in teaching, lecturing, the law, interpreting, careers connected with animals, travel, sports, publishing, writing and even selling. Regardless of your chosen occupation, you are sure to find yourself on many occasions in the right place at the right time, and must be quick to seize these opportunity before somebody else does.

Those of you who have been slaving away towards your chosen goal for many years may actually receive the promotion you so deserve. Yes, Capricorn, this is your year, and it is up to you to make sure you milk every opportunity, until it is sucked dry.

A change of attitude might help too, so try to be more adventurous, think laterally rather than literally and, above all else, use your dry sense of humour to impress prospective employers or clients. It is approximately twelve years since Jupiter was in your sign; think back to this period, realize where you missed out and vow that you will not do so during 1996.

Money Year

As a member of this sign, you need security above all else. A regular pay-packet will give you peace of mind, and this should be remembered whenever you decide to change your career. Any effort to get rich quickly would not normally appeal, and will need to be discouraged if it should. Your way is to proceed steadily on a long-term basis and, when you do, the sky can be the limit and you will not only reach the top of your job, but will enjoy all the material rewards that go with your success.

You know, Capricorn, it is very easy for other people to underestimate you until they know you well or observe you in action over a period of time, because you never push yourself forwards. You would rather take a back seat and from there watch what the opposition is up to. Having done so, you are quick to sense their weaknesses, rush in for the kill and usually emerge a good deal richer. You have a cool, calculating mind that doesn't work with the speed of a Gemini for example, but certainly does outperform most of the other signs when it comes to shrewd, accurate analysis of a financial situation. You are always alert for opportunity. You have a sixth sense for recognizing a chance to swell your bank balance, and you generally take it.

However, both the male and female of this sign can be surprisingly impulsive at times. This is a contradiction in your nature: most of the time you are the epitome of self-discipline, but, quite out of the blue, you perform the rashest acts, blowing some of your hard-earned cash on a possession you have, perhaps, secretly been hankering for over a long period of time. Interestingly, providing this doesn't occur too often, you usually manage to bring back the smile to your bank manager's face. Remember though, there will be many times when Lady Luck will strike during the year ahead, and it is up to you to recognize them and make the most of them.

With erratic Uranus now coasting through the sign of Aquarius, you will have many brilliant ideas on how to swell your bank balance. Do stop and think though; are they really so brilliant or are they just the tiniest bit cranky? Unless you are 100 per cent sure, it would best to wait a while longer before acting.

Still, there is no doubt about it; many Goats will be striking it rich during the year ahead, because Aquarius is the area of your chart which is devoted to money matters, and this sign is, of course, ruled by Uranus. So, the brillance of this planet can go a long way to making you a good deal richer, as long as you never lose sight of common sense. Take your risks by all means, but make sure they are well calculated. In other words, all you have to do is be a typical Capricorn in order to finish up on top.

Love and Sex Year

Your opposite sign of the zodiac is, of course, Cancer, which stands for the feeling and sentimental side of life, the nurturing, protective instinct and all its cherishing emotions. Where you, as a Goat, tend to live in your mind, Cancer is ruled by the heart, and it is from here, across the zodiac, and deep in your subconscious, that come the sudden fanciful impulses which force you to act so uncharacteristically at times. Here, too, is the reservoir of feeling, painfully dammed up by your mental nature. There are times when you can't communicate love and affection. It uses words and symbols for the real thing. Love and affection are implicit, though, in the fire of feelings. A Goat in love can often only manage to express himself or herself properly through sexual acts. You are wonderful at speaking body-to-body language. You are not by nature promiscuous; you need to be in love or to be infatuated to feel real desire. Both sexes of this sign have a reputation for being insatiable in sex; insatiable in love would be more like it.

Whether you want to admit it or not, you need a loving soul-mate. You, more than most people, need a lover who understands your need to pour yourself into a fulfilling career. No one is more energetic or joyful than the Goat who is happy in both work and love. Generally speaking, it is not easy for you to find a compatible partner; one reason being that you are inclined to choose from an intellectual point of view, and are guided by preconceived ideas rather than your emotions. This is probably a good thing because your feelings are rather unreliable and frequently distort your keen perceptions, particularly when they are aroused.

As a rule, you are a cautious lover, and may never succeed in finding the ideal. There is, however, a good chance of finding happiness, if you are ready to accept that everybody has their faults. It is very important that you don't become overcritical of the person you love. Naturally, you may mean well in your efforts to improve him or her, but you can easily give the impression of nagging.

You can also be possessive, which means you will do anything for the person you love, except, perhaps, give him or her sufficient freedom. You are inclined gradually to take the person over. I suppose it would be a good thing for you and your mate to mix a lot, to avoid cutting yourself off too much from other people. Luckily, when it comes to marriage this often inspires you to get out and mix more freely. A loving and understanding partner can help you break old habits.

You are definitely a faithful lover once you have given yourself to someone; you certainly make a bad enemy; you hold off the advances of the opposite sex until you are quite sure of them. Those who offend you usually regret it as they never get a second chance. This is because you have a long and unforgiving memory for insults and disrespect. Still, it has to be said that you are not fanatically vengeful. Certainly, you are prepared to wait, but won't be put out if you never get the opportunity to even the score. There are several distinct advantages in being a Goat, one is that, because you are ruled by Saturn, it is never too late to find love. Therefore, don't put on restrictions or time limits when this experience occur, otherwise you could impulsively rush into a mismatch, which will lead to a great deal of heartache.

What are your chances, then, of finding that special someone during 1996? Well, if you are fancy-free at the beginning of the year, it is likely that you will be content with this status until the period is through. This is mainly due to the fact that Jupiter will be providing you with so many chances to enjoy yourself that you will be most reluctant to give up your precious freedom and devote yourself to one particular person. However, of course, there will be exceptions during this period, and for these you need to look to the *Monthly* and *Daily Guides*. Take note of the phases of the Moon, as these drastically affect your emotions. A Full Moon can bring problems in a relationship to the surface, and could result in the end of the relationship. On the other hand, a New Moon is likely to produce someone exciting and new into your life, so no sitting in front of the television during this period, otherwise you could seriously miss out and that will be a shame.

If you are already married, Jupiter may not be quite such a blessing, as, quite out of character, you could be easily tempted by those sideline attractions. But, should you give in to such temptation, you will eventually realize that it was more painful than pleasurable. This is because you possess a conscience, and find it hard to deceive those you really care about. Flirt by all means; after all, you are only testing your powers of attraction, but make sure the other person understands the signals that you are giving out; otherwise you may find yourself in an embarrassing position more than once during the year ahead. Still, there is one thing that is absolutely certain, and that is that you are not going to be bored.

Health and diet year

The body areas governed by Capricorn are the bones, joints, knees, skin, teeth, nails, hair and gall-bladder. As a Goat, you are prone to stiffness, calcification and chills. It is important for you to try hard to be both physically and mentally flexible. No doubt massage would help to improve your circulation as well as aiding relaxation. Lubrication too, in the form of adequate fluids and the correct natural oils, will keep the body supple and the skin clear.

You are reserved and inclined to distance yourself emotionally from other people, which can be effective in work, but can create barriers in intimate relationships. You need partners who are sensitive and expressive, those who can appreciate your inner warmth, and help you to overcome your shyness. Remember, too, that you have deep feelings that need expression; failure to do this results in your becoming depressed and isolated. Too much self-denial, particularly to personal creativity, is likely to lead to dark moods. Others will be more responsive to you if you can learn to love yourself a little more. Give yourself permission to work less and enjoy life as much as possible.

Like Taurus and Virgo, you are an earth sign, and this is associated with the materialization of earthly dreams and ideals. Like the earth itself, there is a solidarity and physical security about you. Your good health largely depends on good nutrition, and you have a natural instinct as to which foods are right or wrong for you, and you should listen to it.

Earth is also associated with the digestive tract, and it is more likely than any other element to retain some of the impurities from the foods which we consume. You need to use your sense of discrimination when it comes to choosing your diet. Remember, sluggish digestion can lead to an accumulation of waste clogging up your system. Plenty of natural, non-toxic, cleansing foods and pure mineral water will ensure efficient functioning.

It is a good idea to remember that the sign prior to your birthday is frequently a period of lowered resistance and greater susceptibility to germs. This is the time just before the beginning of your new solar year, which represents a lull in the physical life force. Ideally, whilst the Sagittarian period of the year is in operation, you should use this time for spiritual growth, to cleanse and prepare for the year ahead. In doing so, you are likely to live to a ripe old age as many Saturn-born individuals do.

Uranus Life Cycle

Despite the sign that Uranus was in at the time of your birth, following this happy event, each seven year cycle can initiate changes which correspond with the zodiac sequence. For example, the first seven years represent the time between birth and your seventh birthday; this has a distinctive Aries flavour about it. This is followed by the seventh to the fourteenth year period and that has the distinctive Taurus flavour. This procedure is carried on through the Uranus cycle. Now check your age and see whether you are affected by the current cycle that Uranus is in.

0–7 years of age: Arian Phase

This is the period of self-discovery and adventure, when accidents in the form of bumps, minor bruises, burns and cuts are common. It's also a time when kidneys and the bladder are highlighted due to toilet-training, and this can include problems such as bed-wetting; good judgement by parents is important during this phase. Too much discipline during this period can lead later to health conditions of the urinary tract and bowels as well as to rebellion. Naturally, friend-ships are formed at this time too, and a child begins to learn that others exist apart from him or herself.

7–14 years of age: Taurean Phase

This tends to be a time when popularity at school is prominent, as are obsessions and 'crazes'. Fixations on pop stars and other idols, fad foods, and strange dietary habits often occur. Destructive, obsessive behaviour such as nail-biting are other examples of intensity felt during this phase. Because of this, the throat, neck, tonsils, mouth and reproductive system will be areas of sensitivity and curiosity. This is a phase when it is important that a child learns to share in order to feel secure and loved.

14–21 years of age: Geminean Phase

During this period, youngsters are heavily involved in social interaction and learning how to communicate. The hands, arms, shoulders, nerves, sciatic nerve, hips, liver and hormone balance of the body are also emphasized. Mental prowess is tested through writing, reading, examinations and so on, and Dance, music and sport can play a positive recreational role and add balance to those who tend to be over-stressed. This is a time when young people tend to be prone to strain and nervous exhaustion or injury to the limbs. It is also a period when adequate sleep and nourishing diet will help to avoid depressed states.

21–28 years of age: Cancerian Phase

This is a period of growing and nurturing. Many become parents or establish their own 'home'. Despite this it can represent an inner battle between parent and child within all of us. In a perfect world it is a time for 'emotional weaning' from parental dominance, which needs to be tackled, but success depends upon the adaptability of parental influence. Those who do not take control of their own destiny during this phase will be the losers, and may carry resentment around with them until later life.

The digestion and stomach, metabolism, breast, bone structure, teeth and skin are all highlighted at this time.

It is also a stage when we are looking for answers to emotional problems and we tend to overindulge in food and alcohol. It is a time for being objective in difficult situations – and recognizing the fact that life requires work and effort.

28–35 years of age: Leonine Phase

This is an important period where ambition, personal effort, individuality, vocation and a strong contribution to life in relation to other people are all highlighted. There is also an inclination to overdo everything; the heart, circulation, calves, ankles and back are all vulnerable areas at this time. Luckily, recuperative powers are usually good. It tends to be a time when we feel invincible and it must be born in mind that wise choices must be made and sensible priorities taken into consideration.

35–41 years of age: Virgoan Phase

This is a phase when our food tolerance levels are physically tested. Many people begin to reassess their dietary needs, become more health conscious and take positive steps reorganizing their lifestyle to match their changing requirements.

This is a time for mental discrimination. Dislikes and likes are carefully examined; nevertheless, we may still achieve some of our most outstanding work. The spleen, digestive tract, lymphatic system, nervous system and feet may be underlying causes of health problems at this time. Chemical allergies are also a possible source of discomfort, and unpleasant symptoms experienced must be examined.

42–49 years of age: Libran Phase

This phase is frequently labelled the menopause or mid-life crisis and can create a mental or emotional throwback to our childhood. This age celebrates the start of the externalization of the wisdom we have gleaned since birth. If we were given free rein and were thoroughly spoilt during our period of freedom and self-discovery (0–7 years), it will be difficult to adapt to others' needs at this time. Many decide to break away and do things their way at this time. All relationships are tested and often fail; sometimes past relationships are even revived. Adaptability should be the key word during this particular phase. The hormone balance, blood pressure, kidneys and cerebral functions are stressed. Conditions such as dizziness, neuralgia, insomnia and headaches can be helped with the right treatment. The flesh will start to lose its elasticity, but exercise will keep us in trim.

49–56 years of age: Scorpion Phase

Confusing feelings can accompany this period of life. Whilst the 7–14 phase is concerned with developing the reproductive system, this particular part of life is concerned with stabilizing the reproductive system, and generally marks the end of reproduction. The security-consciousness and obsessions emphasized between the ages of 7 and 14 can once again manifest themselves as a fear of aging, possessiveness and obsession with one's sexual prowess or even lack of it. The bowel, bladder, throat, neck and reproductive system all require preventative measures in the form of diet and attitudes.

56–63 years of age: Sagittarian Phase

This period can be extremely rewarding for the person who is involved in living life to the fullest. Great wisdom should have been attained and will help younger friends and family members. Many of this age decide to travel and consider alternative self-improvement activities or education. Others, regrettably, become restless

and bored, develop high cholesterol levels and weight
problems, nervous anxiety and disorders of the blood
and stiffness of the hips and back. During this period
it is important to refocus on personal potentials, to live
a useful and active life, or we may conclude that we
have outlived our usefulness. It's usual at this time for
children to have left home and so we are frequently left
with a void. Now is a time to pick up on hobbies that
have always fascinated us.

63–70 years of age: Capricornian Phase

This can represent a time of achievement, the peak
of a life's work. Many are still productive, but others
retire and look for an alternative occupation or hobby.
It is during this time we reap our health harvest,
which is based on how we have treated our bodies
in the previous years. The effects of calcification and
hardening of joints and arteries may require attention.
Common problems are stones in the organs, hardening
of the joints, drying of the skin and scalp and loss of
teeth and hair. Between the age of 21 and 28 we must
establish our own individuality; between 63 and 70 it
is time to let go of others and allow them to develop
at their own pace. We must not unwittingly hinder the
potential of those we love the most.

70–77 years of age: Aquarian Phase

Oddly enough, new motivations and ambitions often
arise at this time. Often there is a loss of a partner,
so it becomes important to become involved in groups,
in order to establish new friendships and develop new
interests. Unexpected happiness is a distinct possibility, if we remain positive to our circumstances and
seriously consider the contribution we can make. Many
couples in this age group need a refreshing incentive
to share new hobbies, courses and activities involving

intellectual stimulation. A lack of effort can promote lessened muscle co-ordination and absent-mindedness.

77–84 years of age: Piscean Phase

Those in this age group have an inclination to withdraw unless they're wise enough to develop plenty of interests and friends. It is a time of acceptance, sentiment and reflections. Sometimes it is harder for the younger generation to see through the veil of age, because it is frequently disguised by ill-health plus a spirit which is still young, and resents the limitations imposed upon us by our physical conditions. This age group should stick to dramatic dietary modification, especially in the quantity of food eaten – toxic effects are likely through improper absorption of food. The bladder and general vitality are weakened, and bunions are common. Fresh fruit and vegetables and easily digested nutrients combined with pure water can revive, restore and cleanse the body.

84 years of age and later: Second Arian Phase

Those who reach this great age are likely to experience a desire for fresh beginnings. Some even move or marry at this time. Seven-year cycles repeat themselves in what can only be described as a second childhood or, at the very least, as second wind.

(For further information on the various health cycles in life, it is recommended that the reader turns to *The Health Zodiac* by Pamela Row published by Ashgrove Press, 1993).

Numerology Year

In order to discover the number of any year you are
interested in, your 'individual year number', first take
your birth date, day and month, and add this to the year
you are interested in, be it in the past or in the future.
As an example, say you were born on 9 August and you
are interested in 1995:

$$
\begin{array}{r}
9 \\
8 \\
1995 \\
\hline
2012
\end{array}
$$

Then, write down $2 + 0 + 1 + 2$ and you will discover
this equals 5. This means that the number of your
year is 5.

You can experiment with this method by taking any
year from your past and discovering with the help of
the following guide whether or not numerology works
out for you.

The guide is perennial and applicable to all Sun signs:
you can look up years for your friends as well as for
yourself. Use it to discover general trends ahead, the
way you should be approaching a chosen period and
how you can make the most of the future.

INDIVIDUAL YEAR NUMBER 1

GENERAL FEEL

A time for being more self-sufficient and one when you should be ready to grasp the nettle. All opportunities must be snapped up, after careful consideration. Also an excellent time for laying down the foundations for future success in all areas.

DEFINITION

Because this is the number 1 individual year, you will have the chance to start again in many areas of life. The emphasis will be upon the new; there will be fresh faces in your life, more opportunities and perhaps even new experiences. If you were born on either the 1st, 19th or 28th and were born under the sign of Aries or Leo then this will be an extremely important time. It is crucial during this cycle that you be prepared to go it alone, push back horizons and generally open up your mind. Time also for playing the leader or pioneer wherever necessary. If you have a hobby which you wish to turn into a business, or maybe you simply wish to introduce other people to your ideas and plans, then do so whilst experiencing this individual cycle. A great period too for laying down the plans for long-term future gains. Therefore, make sure you do your homework well and you will be reaping the rewards at a later date.

RELATIONSHIPS

This is an ideal period for forming new bonds, perhaps business relationships, new friends and new loves too. You will be attracted to those in high positions and with strong personalities. There may also be an emphasis on bonding with people a good deal younger than yourself. If you are already in a long-standing relationship, then it is time to clear away the dead wood between you which may have been causing misunderstandings and unhappiness. Whether in love or business, you will find those who are born under the sign of Aries, Leo or Aquarius far more common in your life, also those born on the following dates: 1st, 4th, 9th, 10th, 13th, 18th, 19th, 22nd and 28th. The most important months for this individual year when you are likely to meet up with those who have a strong influence on you are January, May, July and October.

CAREER

It is likely that you have been wanting to break free and to explore fresh horizons in your job or in your career and this is definitely a year for doing so. Because you are in a fighting mood, and because your decision-making qualities as well as your leadership qualities are foremost, it will be an easy matter for you to find assistance as well as to impress other people. Major professional changes are likely and you will also feel more independent within your existing job. Should you want times for making important career moves, then choose Mondays or Tuesdays. These are good days for pushing your luck and presenting your ideas well. Changes connected with your career are going to be more likely during April, May, July and September.

HEALTH

If you have forgotten the name of your doctor or dentist, then this is the year for going for check-ups. A time too when people of a certain age are likely to start wearing glasses. The emphasis seems to be on eyes. Start a good health regime. This will help you cope with any adverse events that almost assuredly lie ahead. The important months for your own health as well as for loved ones are March, May and August.

INDIVIDUAL YEAR NUMBER 2

GENERAL FEEL

You will find it far easier to relate to other people.

DEFINITION

What you will need during this cycle is diplomacy, cooperation and the ability to put yourself in someone else's shoes. Whatever you began last year will now begin to show signs of progress. However, don't expect miracles; changes are going to be slow rather than at the speed of light. Changes will be taking place all around you. It is possible too that you will be considering moving from one area to another, maybe even to another country. There is a lively feel about domesticity and in relationships with the opposite sex too. This is going to be a marvellous year for making things come true and asking for favours. However, on no account should you force yourself and your opinions on other people. A spoonful of honey is going to get you a good deal further than a spoonful of vinegar. If you are born under the sign of Cancer or Taurus, or if your birthday falls on the 2nd, 11th, 20th or 29th, then this year is going to be full of major events.

RELATIONSHIPS

You need to associate with other people far more than is usually the case – perhaps out of necessity. The emphasis is on love, friendship and professional partnerships. The opposite sex will be much more prepared to get involved in your life than is normally the case. This is a year your chances of becoming engaged or married are increased and there is likely to be expansion in your family in the form of a lovely addition and also in the families of your friends and those closest to you. The instinctive and caring side to your personality is going to be strong and very obvious. You will quickly discover that you will be extra touchy and sensitive to things that other people say. Further, you will find those born under the sign of Cancer, Taurus and Libra entering your life far more than is usually the case. This also applies to those who are born on the 2nd, 6th, 7th, 11th, 15th, 20th, 24th, 25th or 29th of the month.

Romantic and family events are likely to be emphasized during April, June and September.

CAREER

There is a strong theme of change here, but there is no point in having a panic attack about that because, after all, life is about change. However, in this particular individual year any transformation or upheaval is likely to be of an internal nature, such as at your place of work, rather than external. You may find your company is moving from one area to another, or perhaps there are changes between departments. Quite obviously then the most important thing for you to do in order to make your life easy is to be adaptable. There is a strong possibility too that you may be given added responsibility. Do not flinch, this will bring in extra reward.

If you are thinking of searching for employment this year, then try to arrange all meetings and negotiations on Monday and Friday. These are good days for asking for favours or rises too. The best months are March, April, June, August, and December. All these are important times for change.

HEALTH

This individual cycle emphasizes stomach problems. The important thing for you is to eat sensibly, rather than going on, for example, a crash diet – which could be detrimental. If you are female then you would be wise to have a check-up at least once during the year ahead just to be sure you can continue to enjoy good health. All should be discriminating when dining out. Check cutlery, and take care if food has only been partially cooked. Furthermore, emotional stress could get you down, but only if you allow it. Provided you set aside some periods of relaxation in each day when you can close your eyes and let everything drift away then you will have little to worry about. When it comes to diet, be sure that the emphasis is on nutrition, rather than fighting the flab. Perhaps it would be a good idea to become less weight conscious during this period and let your body find its natural ideal weight on its own. The months of February, April, July and November may show health changes in some way. Common sense is your best guide during this year.

INDIVIDUAL YEAR NUMBER 3

GENERAL FEEL

You are going to be at your most creative and imaginative during this time. There is a theme of expansion and growth and you will want to polish up your self-image in order to make the 'big impression'.

DEFINITION

It is a good year for reaching out, for expansion. Social and artistic developments should be interesting as well as profitable and this will help to promote happiness. There will be a strong urge in you to improve yourself, either your image or your reputation or perhaps your mind. Your popularity soars through the ceiling and this delights you. Involving yourself with something creative brings increased success plus a good deal of satisfaction. However, it is imperative that you keep

yourself in a positive mood. This will attract attention
and appreciation of all of your talents. Projects which
were begun two years ago are likely to be sprouting
this year. If you are born under the sign of Pisces or
Sagittarius, or your birthday falls on the 3rd, 12th, 21st
or 30th, then this year is going to be particularly special
and successful.

RELATIONSHIPS

There is a happy-go-lucky feel about all your relationships and you are in a flirty, fancy-free mood.
Heaven help anyone trying to catch you during the
next twelve months: they will need to get their skates
on. Relationships are likely to be ethereal and fun
rather than heavy going. It is possible too that you
will find yourself with those who are younger than you,
particularly those born under the signs of Pisces and
Sagittarius, and those whose birth dates add up to 3, 6
or 9. Your individual cycle shows important months for
relationships are March, May, August and December.

CAREER

As I discussed earlier, this individual number is one
that suggests branching out and personal growth, so be
ready to take on anything new. Not surprisingly, your
career aspects look bright and shiny. You are definitely
going to be more ambitious and must keep up that
positive façade and attract opportunities. Avoid taking
obligations too flippantly; it is important that you adopt
a conscientious approach to all your responsibilities.
You may take on a fresh course of learning or look for a
new job, and the important days for doing so would be
on Thursday and Friday: these are definitely your best
days. This is particularly true in the months of February,
March, May, July and November: expect expansion in
your life and take a chance during these times.

HEALTH

Because you are likely to be out and about painting the town all the colours of the rainbow, it is likely that some of your health problems could come through over-indulgence or perhaps tiredness. However, if you have got to have some health problems, I suppose these are the best ones to experience, because they are under your control. There is also a possibility that you may get a little fraught over work, which may result in some emotional scenes. However, you are sensible enough to realize they should not be taken too seriously. If you are prone to skin allergies, then these too could be giving you problems during this particular year. The best advice you can follow is not to go to extremes that will affect your body or your mind. It is all very well to have fun, but after a while too much not only affects your health but also the degree of enjoyment you experience. Take extra care between January and March, and June and October, especially where these are winter months for you.

INDIVIDUAL YEAR NUMBER 4

GENERAL FEEL

It is back to basics this year. Do not build on shaky foundations. Get yourself organized and be prepared to work a little harder than you usually do and you will come through without any great difficulty.

DEFINITION

It is imperative this year that you have a grand plan. Do not simply rush off without considering the consequences and avoid dabbling of all descriptions. It is likely too that you will be gathering more responsibility and on occasions this could lead you to feeling unappreciated, claustrophobic and perhaps over-burdened in some ways. Although it is true to say that this cycle in your individual life tends to bring about a certain amount of limitation, whether this be on the personal side to life, the psychological or the financial, you now have the chance to get yourself together and to build on more solid foundations. Security is definitely your key word at this time. When it comes to any project, or job or plan, it is important that you ask the right questions. In other words, do your homework before you go off half cock. That would be a disaster. If you are an Aquarius, a Leo or a Gemini or you are born on the 4th, 13th, 22nd, or the 31st of any month, this individual year will be extremely important and long remembered.

RELATIONSHIPS

You will find that it is the eccentric, the unusual, the unconventional, the downright odd, that will be drawn into your life during this particular cycle. It is also strongly possible that people you have not met for some time may be re-entering your circle and an older person or somebody outside your own social or perhaps religious background will be drawn to you too. When it comes to the romantic side of things, again you are drawn to that which is different from usual. You may even form a relationship with someone who comes from a totally different background, perhaps from a distance. Something unusual about them stimulates and excites you. Gemini, Leo and Aquarius are your likely favourites, as well as anyone whose birth number adds up to 1, 4, 5, or 7. Certainly the most exciting months for romance are going to be February, April, July and November. Make sure then that you put yourself about during this particular time, and be ready for literally anything.

CAREER

Once more we have the theme of the unusual and different in this area of life. You may be plodding along in the same old rut when suddenly lightning strikes and you find yourself besieged by offers from other people and in a panic, not quite sure what to do. There may be a period when nothing particular seems to be going on, when to your astonishment you are given some promotion or some exciting challenge to take on board. Literally anything can happen in this particular cycle of your life. The individual year 4 also inclines towards added responsibilities and it is important that you do not offload them on to other people or cringe in fear. They will eventually pay off and in the meantime you will be gaining in experience and paving the way for greater success in the future. When you want to arrange any kind of meeting, negotiation or perhaps ask for any kind of favour at work, then try to do so on a Monday or a Wednesday for the luckiest results. January, February, April, October and November are certainly the months when you must play the opportunist and be ready to say yes to anything that comes your way.

HEALTH

The biggest problems that you will have to face this year are caused by stress, so it is important that you attend to your diet and are as philosophical as possible as well as ready to adapt to changing conditions. You are likely to find that people you thought you knew well are acting out of character and this throws you off balance. Take care too when visiting the doctor. Remember that you are dealing with a human being and that doctors, like the rest of us, can make mistakes. Unless you are 100 per cent satisfied then go for a second opinion over anything important. Try to be sceptical about yourself too because you are going to be a good deal more moody than usual. The times that need special attention are February, May, September and November. If any of these months fall in the winter part of your year, then wrap up well and dose up on vitamin C.

INDIVIDUAL YEAR NUMBER 5

GENERAL FEEL

There will be many more opportunities for you to get out and about and travel is certainly going to be playing a large part in your year. Change too must be expected and even embraced – after all, it is part of life. You will have more free time and choices, so all in all things look promising.

DEFINITION

It is possible that you tried previously to get something off the launching pad but for one reason or another, it simply didn't happen. Luckily, you now get a chance to renew those old plans and put them into action. You are certainly going to feel that things are changing for the better in all areas. You are going to be more actively involved with the public and will enjoy a certain amount of attention and publicity. You may have failed in the past but this year mistakes will be easier to accept and learn from, and you are going to find yourself both physically and mentally more in tune with your environment and with those you care about than ever before. If you are a Gemini or a Virgo or are born on the 5th, 14th or 23rd then this is going to be a period of major importance for you and you must be ready to take advantage of this.

RELATIONSHIPS

Lucky you! Your sexual magnetism goes through the ceiling and you will be involved in many relationships during the year ahead. You have that extra charisma about you which will be drawing others to you and you can look forward to being choosy. There will be an inclination to be drawn to those who are considerably younger than yourself. It is likely too that you will find that those born under the signs of Taurus, Gemini, Virgo and Libra as well as those whose birth date adds up to 2, 5 or 6 will play an important part in your year. The months for attracting others in a big way are January, March, June, October and December.

CAREER

This is considered by all numerologists as being one of the best numbers for self-improvement in all areas, and particularly on the professional front. It will be relatively easy for you to sell your ideas and yourself as well as to push your skills and expertise under the noses of other people. They will certainly sit up and notice. Clearly, then, a time for you to view the world as though it were your oyster and to get out there and grab your slice of the action. You have increased confidence and should be able to get exactly what you want. Friday and Wednesday are perhaps the best days if looking for a job or going to negotiations or interviews, or in fact for generally pushing yourself into the limelight. Watch out for March, May, September, October or December. Something of great importance could pop up at this time. There will certainly be a chance for advancement; whether you take it up or not is of course entirely up to you.

HEALTH

Getting a good night's rest could be your problem during the year ahead, since that mind of yours is positively buzzing and won't let you rest. Try turning your brain off at bedtime, otherwise you will finish up irritable and exhausted. Try to take things a step at a time without rushing around. Meditation may help you to relax and do more for your physical wellbeing than anything else. Because this is an extremely active year, you will need to do some careful planning so that you can cope with ease rather than rushing around like a demented mayfly. Furthermore, try to avoid going over the top with alcohol, food, sex, gambling or anything which could be described as 'get rich quick'. During January, April, August, and October, watch yourself a bit, you could do with some coddling, particularly if these happen to be winter months for you.

INDIVIDUAL YEAR NUMBER 6

GENERAL FEEL

There is likely to be increased responsibility and activity within your domestic life. There will be many occasions when you will be helping loved ones and your sense of duty is going to be strong.

DEFINITION

Activities for the most part are likely to be centred around property, family, loved ones, romance and your home. Your artistic appreciation will be good and you will be drawn to anything that is colourful and beautiful, and possessions that have a strong appeal to your eye or even your ear. Where domesticity is concerned, there is a strong suggestion that you may move out of one home into another. This is an excellent time too for self-education, for branching out, for graduating, for taking on some extra courses – whether simply to improve your appearance or to improve your mind. When it comes to your social life you are inundated with chances to attend social functions, such as openings of art galleries and facilities. You are going to be the real social butterfly flitting from scene to scene and enjoying yourself thoroughly. Try to accept nine out of ten invitations that come your way because they bring with them chances of advancement. If you are born on the 6th, 15th or 24th or should your birth sign be Taurus, Libra or Cancer then this is going to be a year that will be long remembered as a very positive one.

RELATIONSHIPS

When it comes to love, sex and romance the individual year 6 is perhaps the most successful. It is a time for being swept off your feet, for becoming engaged or for getting married. On the more negative side, perhaps there is a separation and divorce. However the latter can be avoided, provided you are prepared to sit down and communicate properly. There is an emphasis too on pregnancy and birth, or changes in existing relationships. Circumstances will be sweeping you along. If you are born under the sign of Taurus, Cancer or Libra, then it is even more likely that this will be a major year for you, as well as for those born on dates adding up to 6, 3 or 2. The most memorable months of your year are going to be February, May, September and November. Grab all opportunities to enjoy yourself and improve your relationships during these periods.

CAREER

A good year for this side to life too, with the chances of promotion and recognition for past efforts all coming your way. You will be able to improve your position in life even though lately it is likely you have been frustrated. On the cash front big rewards will come flooding in mainly because you are prepared to fulfil your obligations and commitments without complaint or protest. Other people will appreciate all the efforts you have put in, so plod along and you will find your efforts will not be in vain. Perversely, if you are looking for a job or setting up an interview, negotiation or a meeting, or simply want to advertise your talents in some way, then your best days for doing so are Monday, Thursday and Friday. Long-term opportunities are very strong during the months of February, April, August, September and November. These are the key periods for pushing yourself up the ladder of success.

HEALTH

If you are to experience any problems of a physical nature during this year, then they could be tied up with the throat, nose or the tonsils plus the upper parts of the body. Basically what you need to stay healthy during this year is plenty of sunlight, moderate exercise, fresh air and changes of scene. Escape to the coast too if this is at all possible. The months for being particularly watchful are March, July, September and December. Think twice before doing anything during this time and there is no reason why you shouldn't stay hale and hearty for the whole year.

INDIVIDUAL YEAR NUMBER 7

GENERAL FEEL

A year for inner growth and for finding out what really makes you tick and what you need to make you happy.

Self-awareness and discovery are all emphasized during the individual year 7.

DEFINITION

You will be provided with the opportunity to place as much emphasis as possible on your personal life and your own wellbeing. There will be many occasions when you will find yourself analysing your past motives and actions, and developing a need to give more attention to your own personal needs, goals and desires. There will also be many occasions when you will feel the need to escape any kind of confusion, muddle or noise, and time spent alone will not be wasted. It will give you time for meditation and also for examining exactly where you have come to so far and where you want to go in the future. It is important you make up your mind what you want out of this particular year because once you have done this you will attain those ambitions. Failure to do so could mean you end up chasing your tail and that is a pure waste of time and energy. You will also discover that secrets about yourself and other people could be surfacing during this year. If you are born under the sign of Pisces or Cancer, or on the 7th, 16th or 25th of the month, then this year will be especially wonderful.

RELATIONSHIPS

It has to be said from the word go that this is not the best year for romantic interest. A strong need for contemplation will mean spending time on your own. Any romance that does develop this year may not live up to your great expectations, but, providing you are prepared to take things as they come without jumping to conclusions, then you will enjoy yourself without getting hurt. Decide exactly what it is you have in mind and then go for it. Romantic interests this year are likely to be with people who are born on dates that add up to 2, 4 or 7 or with people born under the sign of Cancer or Pisces. Watch for romantic opportunities during January, April, August and October.

CAREER

When we pass through this particular individual cycle, two things in life tend to occur: retirement from the limelight, or a general slowing down, perhaps by taking leave of absence or maybe retraining in some way. It is likely too that you will become more aware of your own occupational expertise and skills – you will begin to understand your true purpose in life and will feel much more enlightened. Long-sought-after goals begin to come to life if you have been drifting of late. The best attitude to have throughout the year is an exploratory one when it comes to your work. If you want to set up negotiations, interviews or meetings, arrange them for Monday or Friday. In fact any favours you seek should be tackled on these days. January, March, July, August, October and December are particularly good for self-advancement.

HEALTH

Since, in comparison to previous years, this is a rather quiet time, health problems are likely to be minor. Some will possibly come through irritation or worry and the best thing to do is to attempt to remain meditative and calm. This state of mind will bring positive results. Failure to do so may create unnecessary problems by allowing your imagination to run completely out of control. You need time this year to restore, recuperate and contemplate. Any health changes that do occur are likely to happen in February, June, August and November.

INDIVIDUAL YEAR NUMBER 8

GENERAL FEEL

This is going to be a time for success, for making important moves and changes, a time when you may gain power and certainly one when your talents are going to be recognized.

DEFINITION

This individual year gives you the chance to 'think big', a time you can occupy the limelight and wield power. If you were born on the 8th, 17th or 26th of the month or come under the sign of Capricorn, pay attention to this year and make sure you make the most of it. You should develop greater maturity and will discover a true feeling of faith and destiny, both in yourself and in events that occur. This is a cycle connected with career, ambition and money, but debts from the past will have to be re-paid. For example, an old responsibility or debt that you may have avoided in past years may reappear to haunt you. However, whatever you do with this twelve months, aim high – think big, think success and above all be positive.

RELATIONSHIPS

This particular individual year is one which is strongly connected with birth, divorce and marriage – most of the landmarks we experience in life in fact. Lovewise, those who are more experienced or older than you, or someone of power, authority, influence or wealth will be very attractive. This year will be putting you back in touch with those from your past – old friends, comrades, associates, and even romances from long ago crop up once more. You should not experience any great problems romantically this year, especially if you are dealing with Capricorns or Librans, or with those whose date of birth adds up to 8, 6 or 3. The best months for romance to develop are likely to be March, July, September and December.

CAREER

The number 8 year is generally believed to be the best one when it comes to bringing in cash. It is also good for asking for a rise or achieving promotion or authority over other people. This is your year for bathing in the limelight of success, the result perhaps of your past efforts. Now you will be rewarded. Financial success is all but guaranteed, provided you keep faith with your ambitions and yourself. It is important that you set major aspirations for yourself and work slowly towards them. You will be surprised how easily they are fulfilled. Conversely, if you are looking for work, then do set up interviews, negotiations and meetings, preferably on Saturday, Thursday or Friday, which are your luckiest days. Also watch out for chances to do yourself a bit of good during February, June, July, September and November.

HEALTH

You can avoid most health problems, particularly headaches, constipation or liver problems, by avoiding moods of depression, and feelings of loneliness. It is important when these descend that you keep yourself busy enough not to dwell on them. When it comes to receiving attention from the medical profession you would be well advised to get a second opinion. Eat wisely, try to keep a positive and enthusiastic outlook on life and all will be well. Periods which need special care are January, May, July and October. Therefore, if these months fall during the winter part of your year, wrap up and dose yourself with vitamins.

INDIVIDUAL YEAR NUMBER 9

GENERAL FEEL

A time for tying up the loose ends. Wishes are likely to be fulfilled and matters brought to swift conclusions. Inspirations run amok. Much travel is likely.

DEFINITION

The number 9 individual year is perhaps the most successful of all. It tends to represent the completion of matters and affairs, whether in work, business, or personal affairs. Your ability to let go of habits, people and negative circumstances or situations, that may have been holding you back, is strong. The sympathetic and humane side to your character also surfaces and you learn to give more freely of yourself without expecting anything in return. Any good deeds that you do will certainly be well rewarded, in terms of satisfaction and perhaps financially too. If you are born under the sign of Aries or Scorpio, or on the 9th, 18th or 27th of the month, this is certainly going to be an all important year.

RELATIONSHIPS

The individual year 9 is a cycle which gives appeal as well as influence. Because of this, you will be getting emotionally tied up with members of the opposite sex who may be outside your usual cultural or ethnic group. The reason for this is that this particular number relates to humanity and of course this tends to quash ignorance, pride and bigotry. You also discover that Aries, Leo and Scorpio people are going to be much more evident in your domestic affairs, as well as those whose birth dates add up to 9, 3 or 1. The important months for relationships are February, June, August and November. These will be extremely hectic and eventful from a romantic viewpoint and there are times when you could be swept off your feet.

CAREER

This is a year which will help to make many of your dreams and ambitions come true. Furthermore it is an excellent time for success if you are involved in marketing your skills, your talents and your expertise on a broader level. You may be thinking of expanding abroad for example and if so this is certainly a good idea. You will find that harmony and cooperation with your co-workers or those who work for you are easier than before and this will help your dreams and ambitions. The best days for you if you want to line up meetings or negotiations are going to be Tuesday and Thursday and this also applies if you are looking for employment or want a special day for doing something of an ambitious nature. Employment or business changes could also feature during January, May, June, August and October.

HEALTH

The only physical problem you may have during this particular year is accidents, so be careful. Try too to avoid unnecessary tension and arguments with other people. Take extra care when you are on the roads: no drinking and driving for example. You will only have problems if you play your own worst enemy. Be extra watchful when in the kitchen or bathroom: sharp instruments that you find in these areas can lead to cuts being commonplace, unless you take care.

Monthly Guide

JANUARY

With no less than four planets in your sign for the majority of the month, it is certainly a time for pushing ahead with all self-interest. Your confidence has increased, and your warmth will attract other people to you. Mars, the planet of enterprise, initiative, passion and sex, squats in your sign during the first week, so expect the sap to be rising around this time, but do try to stay out of trouble if you are in an existing relationship.

Workwise, it is an ideal time for the freelancer or self-employed. Those in uniformed occupations need to make important moves during the first week. This is a time when confidence is at its highest, and so it is very much a case of actions speaking louder than words, if you are to make the sort of progress that you desire.

Venus' placing in Aquarius during the first fourteen days will be throwing a rosy glow over finances; because of this you are likely to be spending on minor luxuries, fine clothes and maybe on romance.

Mercury is in Aquarius from the 2nd to the 17th and is certainly lucky for those who are involved in sales, the media or publishing, during the first eight days of the month. However after this Mercury decides to go into retrograde movement, so contracts and paperwork could become unbelievably complicated. Think twice before signing on the dotted line during this period. Luckily, this mischievous planet sees common sense on the 30th and, once this occurs, you can then push ahead with travel matters, the law and confidently sign on that dotted line.

Emotionally, you seem to be more in love with your bank balance than any member of the opposite sex. Although, if there is a tidy sum tucked away underneath their mattress, you might just be able to arouse a certain amount of interest.

Luckily, matters change slightly after the 14th, when Venus moves into the sign of Pisces. Don't expect anything fantastic to occur overnight; it is simply that you are beginning a few weeks when there will be many opportunities for romance, but nothing lasting, I am afraid. Still, at least this placing will allow you to feel more at ease with yourself, and will incline you to be much more sociable and gregarious. It won't do any harm either to those of you who are creative. Good and original ideas dash through your brain and you need to keep a pen and pad handy. Should you be professionally involved in sales or the media, it might be a good idea to mix business with pleasure whenever possible, in order to get the maximum out of this month.

Physically, and healthwise in particular, do try to take it easy during the first week of the month. There will be a natural tendency for you to try and catch up on work that has been left undone and, in doing so, you could grind yourself down. What is more, be extra vigilant where hot and sharp objects are concerned, and try to control impulse when you are driving. Always remember that the roads were not built exclusively for you. Should you fail to bear this in mind, you can expect the odd prang or two. However, all in all, this is your month; it comes once a year

and it really is a time when you should be ready
to go after whatever or whoever you want out of
life. All you need to do in order to achieve your
ambitions is to believe that it is possible. Once you
have banished negative thinking, nothing and nobody
can hold you back. Remember, you are the strongest
and most determined sign of the zodiac; bear this in
mind at all times, and it will help to propel you up
the ladder of success. Now for a look at the state of
the Moon.

The Full Moon occurs in the sign of Cancer on 5
January. It is of course your opposite sign, so it could
stir up some discontentment in an existing relationship.
It may even come to an end if you push your luck
too much. Mind you, if you are looking for a reason
to terminate an unsatisfactory emotional attachment,
this is the time for leaping into action. Remember
too, that, like Cancer, you are often affected by the
Full Moon and, if you find yourself imagining the
worst or suffering from that feeling of 'down in the
dumps', try not to take yourself too seriously; accept
the fact that it is only the Full Moon stirring you up.
Then you are halfway towards conquering this state
of mind.

The New Moon this month occurs on 20 January and
falls in your sign. Time for painting on a broader
canvas or taking one or two chances, and, above all
else, for taking on new ideas and situations. Fresh
faces are likely to appear on your scene and new
romances are frequently launched at the time of the
New Moon. Don't hide yourself away then, Capricorn;
it is no time to be reclusive. Put yourself about a
bit, put a smile on your face, and you will find the
opposite sex thinks you positively irresistible. Not a
bad month, but, of course, it is up to you to make the
most of it.

FEBRUARY

Some astrologers associate the 'miser' with the sign of
Capricorn. But, whilst this particular astrologer is willing to admit that you certainly can do a fair imitation of
Scrooge when in the right frame of mind, this is by no
means your usual mode of behaviour. Having said this,
it must be admitted that during this particular month,
the emphasis is definitely on cash, and, the position of
the Sun in Aquarius, suggests you will be reluctant to
do anything for nothing. You will expect to be rewarded
for all your efforts, but perhaps this is only fair. You
will certainly be counting the pennies though; there is
no denying that, and, because of this, it is an excellent
time for those who work with cash, in banking, in
insurance or any monetary profession. It is good, too,
for Goats who wish to approach such people, as I think
you will find them eager to listen and help in any way
they can. Mind you, during the first two weeks, Mars
does lurk in the financial area of life. Because of this, of
you need to hang on tightly to those possessions and
avoid impulse buying. Be especially watchful of your
purse or your wallet when in crowds. Be alert 'there is
a thief about' is very apt during this time. But, and it
is a big but, this is only a possibility and nothing that
a little extra caution can't easily dispel in record time.

For the first two weeks of the month, Mercury will
be lurking in your sign; this will stir you up both
physically and mentally, and you may find it more
than usually difficult to sit still for any length of time.
However, if you a professional traveller then so much
the better. Paperwork, including documents, may also
be of great importance during this period and, certainly,
if you are expecting to deal with important papers, or
even add your signature to them, then you couldn't
have picked a more propitious time. This planet, of

course, is also associated with travel, and so any chance to keep on the move will be snapped up as you will be feeling much more restless than is usually the case. Many of you, too, will be going in for a bout of self-improvement and may enrol in some kind of course, perhaps in an effort to improve your chances of employment and, at the same time, you will be meeting many new people.

During the first week, Venus will be squatting in the sign of Pisces and you will be meeting many exciting prospects which will be setting that heart of yours fluttering. But, don't get too carried away, as disillusionment is likely to follow any attachments made at this time, so keep it casual, Capricorn. From the 14th onwards, Mars moves into the watery sign of Pisces, and, because of this, you will get the message. This planet, of course, represents sex and physical attraction and, luckily, you recognize that it is only your hormones that are stirring you up, and anyone new you may meet is certainly not going to be the love of your life. But be careful – it isn't wise to take chances during this day and age. This placing will also stir your brain cells to be a little more impulsive than is usually the case, which won't only affect your sex life, but also the way in which you conduct yourself on the working front. Should you believe that somebody is taking advantage of you, then you certainly won't be slow to say so. It would be a good idea to couch your words in a certain amount of charm, rather than being too abrasive, because it won't pay to make enemies at this time.

Socially, invitations are likely to roll in from people who are acquaintances rather than from friends who seem to be otherwise engaged. Don't be afraid to take the plunge and meet new people. You will be surprised how revitalizing they can be. And some may even change your outlook or approach to life. The position of Mars is also likely to make you more impatient when travelling, particularly when driving. So try and stay calm, allow plenty of time to get to your destination, wherever that may be, and you will be minimizing this effect.

Certainly, February doesn't promise to be the most exciting month of your life, but it is full of activity and chances for enjoying yourself, be they only fleeting. Be sure then that you play as hard as you work, and you will be creating a nice balance in your life which will help to maintain a shiny coat and a wet nose. Now for a look at the state of the Moon.

The Full Moon this month occurs in the sign of Leo on 4 February. A warning, if ever there was one, to stay on the right side of the law, and to be respectful of officials and bureaucrats, no matter how much you may be sorely tempted to give them a piece of your mind. Certainly, at the moment it is unlikely you can spare it. Many of you who have been mulling over whether or not to continue with a particular relationship may suddenly reach the conclusion that it is a complete waste of time and so will bring it to a swift demise. Having done so, it is likely that you will breathe a great sigh of relief. The New Moon, this month, occurs in the airy sign of Aquarius on 18 February. And, during this day, in fact the whole New Moon period, there is a strong possibility of a fresh source of income presenting itself, and you must be quick to snap it up. It is likely, too, that you will be gaining a brand new possession which you are particularly proud of, perhaps some kind of status symbol. This is an excellent time for taking all financial decisions, because your head is clear and you are thinking positively, so mistakes will be most unlikely. For a more in-depth look at this period, please refer to the *Daily Guide*.

MARCH

Should you want to make any minor adjustments to your financial affairs or deal with any kind of paperwork, then try to do so between the 1st and 6th when Mercury will be squatting in the financial area of your chart. After this it moves on into the sign of Pisces and will bring with it several chances for you to go on short trips either social, romantic or business. Certainly, you are going to be on the go far more than is usually the case, and will find all this increased activity extremely stimulating, mentally as well as physically.

Workwise, those of you involved in sales, the media or publishing should be doing extremely well, although, the presence of Mars in Pisces will mean you should expect to work hard for your pay-packet, not that this will faze a determined character like your good self. You also seem to have a fund of mental energy, certainly up until the 24th anyway. It will be a good idea to think things through as there is a tendency for you to be mentally impulsive, and what initially seems to be a sure-fire winner, could, a couple of days later, appear to be rather foolhardy.

Should you need a time for sorting out differences between members of the family, try to choose the first week, when Venus is squatting in the fiery sign of Aries, because this will help to create harmony between yourself and relatives and incline them to be more open-minded to ideas and suggestions. This is a good time for entertaining at home or considering some kind of home improvement, because there will be a strong urge in you to beautify those surroundings of yours. As usual, you will be out there looking for a bargain, and it won't be difficult to locate.

Once Venus enters Taurus on the 5th it is very much a case of the 'good times' are upon you. Venus will be making you flirty and sociable, and helping the Goat who is either artistic or sporty. Emotionally though, don't take yourself too seriously. You seem to be confronted by an array of attractive faces and are spoiled for choice. Should this be the case, give any commitment at all, try to fit everybody in so that you may take your time without ignoring someone of true value. Really then, this isn't a time for others or even yourself to take your emotional reactions too seriously. This, of course, could be something of a drawback if you already happen to be married. That partner of yours is not going to be pleased, and you should do your best to exercise a little self-control. You have plenty; it is just a matter of whether you want to use it. Socially, this is one of the best months of the year; others are clamouring for your company; and, though you are not madly keen on parties, just for once, you are prepared to play the giddy Goat and accept any chance for having fun which is presented to you.

If you are a parent, March is an ideal month for sorting out problems between yourself and children, because they are more prepared to sit down and listen to what you have to say, which is because you are expressing yourself in a charming, caring and nurturing fashion.

Financially, Mercury will be squatting in Aquarius during the first week suggesting minor expenses and gains, but nothing too drastic. Mind you, paperwork could lead to financial gains, so read documents and contracts very carefully.

Mars will continue in the sign of Pisces up until the 24th. There remains the slight danger of prangs whilst out on short trips. Try to observe some kind of courtesy on the roads and you will find this easy to avoid. Now for a look at the state of the Moon.

The Full Moon this month occurs in the earthy sign

of Virgo after 5 March. There is a suggestion here
then that you should be extra courteous when in the
company of strangers, particularly if they come from
abroad. A wrong word or unthinking gesture could
lead to great offence. If it is necessary for you to go on
any long-distance journeys, then have no fear, but do
double check everything; you don't want to be getting
off at one airport when you should be at another. Also
double check all other documents and arrangements.

The New Moon during March occurs in the watery
sign of Pisces on the 19th. Quite unexpectedly, you may
be asked to make a professional visit or trip. Good ideas
abound at this time and you should take them seriously, because amongst them could be a 'winner'. Brief
encounters of an emotional nature are likely to occur at
this time too, and any new relationship begun, whether
it be personal, emotional or professional, is likely to be
long-lasting and extremely profitable. March seems to
be a month to look forward to in more ways than one.

APRIL

One of the most important astrological events of this
particular month is that Saturn will have finished its
sojourn through Pisces after the 6th. It will then be
entering the fiery sign of Aries and this is likely to affect
your personality, because you will be inclined occasionally to adopt the Ram's attitude to life, particularly
when this planet is aspected by another. This means
you might be more headstrong and impatient, but at
the same time more enterprising, warm-hearted and
go-getting. Pay especial attention to the *Daily Guide* and
the aspects with Saturn. This planet's actual placing in
Aries is devoted to the area of life concerning property
and family, so it looks as if you may be gathering some

extra responsibilities – as if you need any more – over the next couple of years. Never mind, this may come in the delightful form of an addition to the family; or perhaps a new home which requires a good deal of hard work, by which you are certainly not in the least bit intimidated. Naturally then, if you happen to work in property or its allied trades, it is going to be a hectic as well as profitable month. Socially, there will be a natural inclination for you to prefer to entertain on your own stamping grounds, but you can overdo it. And, if I were you, I would certainly force myself out into the big wide world on occasions; otherwise you could become a little stodgy in your thinking. Venus, for example, is encouraging you to mix business with pleasure more than is usually the case, and you are sure to find the company of colleagues a sheer delight and their sense of humour utterly irresistible.

Emotionally, you need to be a little careful, particularly if you are married, as there may be a strong attraction springing up between yourself and someone on the working front. Nothing wrong with this, of course, if you are single, but if not, the grey clouds of trouble could be gathering over your head. Use that wonderful common sense of yours, and it will save you a great deal of trouble, and perhaps money, in the near future.

Healthwise, Venus' move into Gemini from the 3rd onwards will certainly be encouraging you into excesses. Overeating and drinking could lay you low on occasions. Of course, you may decide the price is well worth paying, and that is entirely up to you. Still, it might be worth you taking some time out to decide whether or not you can afford to throw your money away like this. If the answer is 'yes', then full steam ahead and never mind the consequences.

For the entire month, Mars will be squatting in its own sign of Aries which could be creating a certain amount of tension between yourself and relatives. There will be times when you will be tempted to be abrasive with a member of your clan, but, if you are wise, you will bite your tongue, as it will become necessary for you to apologize at a later date, and this isn't something that is easy for a proud person like you.

Now for a look at the state of the Moon. The Full Moon this month occurs on 4 April in the airy sign of Gemini. A further indication that you may not have as much energy at your disposal as is normally the case. Try to take it easy during the Full Moon period, pace yourself, and in that way you will stay hale and hearty. It will also be a good idea not to antagonize workmates unnecessarily, as they are hypersensitive at this time, and, to your embarrassment, could burst either into temper tantrums or into tears at the slightest criticism.

The New Moon this month occurs in the sign of Aries once more the home and property area to life. A minor new cycle seems to be going on and there may be some pleasant news connected with the family. As always, New Moons should be used for making fresh starts in any area you choose. All in all, April seems to hold a good deal of promise. For further information please refer to the *Daily Guide*.

MAY

With no less than five planets in retrograde movement, which means that from our position in space they appear to be going backwards, you can be quite sure that it is very much a case of, if all those around you are losing their heads, then for heaven's sake hang on to yours. Yes, life could become unduly complicated in many areas, but, with a calm approach there is nothing you cannot successfully handle.

Luckily, for most of the month, the Sun will be squatting with Mars in the earthy sign of Taurus. Certainly, you can expect a hard-working period if you work with children, in the arts or sports. However, there will be plenty of chances for you to enjoy yourself, in fact perhaps too many. Try to ensure that you get in one or two early nights, otherwise you could finish up on the sick-list.

Mercury's placing in Taurus seems to suggest that you may develop a sudden interest of an intellectual, rather than a physical nature. Perhaps somebody is introducing you to chess, backgammon or something similar. Whatever it is, you are certainly a keen convert.

If you are a family person, the activity of children may not altogether meet with your approval, and they may need a gentle reprimand; much, of course, depends on age. If you happen to be dealing with teenagers, treat them like adults in order to get the best results.

Emotionally, there still continues an inclination for you to be extremely flirty in your place of work. Nothing, of course, wrong with testing out your powers of attraction, but they might be working too well, and, if you happen to be married, this could land you in hot water right up to your neck.

The lucky professions for the month are those connected with the service industries, health, sports and arts. If you are out of work, but trained in these areas, step up your efforts as they can be made to pay off.

Cashwise, Uranus is now in retrograde movement and you need to make sure you get value for money when out shopping, or when booking a holiday. Carelessness in any direction will leave you all the poorer later on in the year, and this is something that is easily avoidable.

You seem to be extremely active, but if you are taking

part in sports, watch out for strains and sprains, which are a real threat if you are too impulsive. Tiredness and exhaustion may also be out to get you because you are overdoing the late night scene. Luckily, you have the constitution of an ox, or should I say a Goat, and seem to be able to work and play hard with little effort, well, for most of the time. A bit of a mixed month then. Now let's have a look at the state of the Moon.

The Moon is full on 3 May in the watery sign of Scorpio, a time when you need to tread very carefully and diplomatically where the feelings of your friends are concerned. One wrong word and somebody important to you could 'exit stage right', before you have had a chance to apologize. As always, Full Moons can affect your personal relationships, and, if someone close to you becomes unusually moody or unreasonable, it is perhaps best to shrug your shoulders and ignore it for the time being, unless, of course, you think they are attention-seeking, in which case you should give them what they want, lots and lots of lovely attention.

The New Moon this month falls in the earthy sign of Taurus on the 17th, which is, of course, the fun area of life. Perhaps then an exciting invitation is winging its way in your direction. For some Goats, though, this could lead to a brief but passionate affair. Whatever way you look at it there seems to be lots to look forward to. If you are at all creative then one of your projects is likely to be accepted, and this is sure to delight, not only you, but everybody closest to you.

JUNE

On a professional level, this is definitely a month for those of you who are involved in the service industries or any area which is devoted to physical well-being and health. For other Goats it is a time for routine work, nothing too flamboyant or outrageous. Good then for putting the finishing touches to projects and maybe making plans for the future.

Healthwise, there continues the tendency for you to overdo it where food and drink are concerned, but you have plenty of splendid self-control, so there really isn't any excuse. Naturally, if you have decided to treat your body in this way, you must expect it to protest at a later date, so do try to be sensible. The placing of Mercury and Mars in Taurus for most of the month certainly makes life hectic for those of you who are creative or working with children. Social life, too, receives a shot in the arm, and you will be meeting many new people, some of whom will have heads bursting full of ideas which you can use to your own benefit in some way during the future.

If you are a family person with children, do try to protect them from overdoing it. It is likely that youngsters are trying to pack too much action into their days or even their nights, and, as a result, could finish on a sick-list. A quiet word in their ear can easily prevent this state of affairs.

Cashwise, whilst Uranus remains in retrograde action, there is a danger of money matters becoming unduly complicated and, because of this, you need to try to offset such a trend by being straightforward in all your dealings. Any inclination towards being devious or too clever by half could land you in hot water. Be your usual sensible self, and you will have little to fear.

Now Pluto is in retrograde movement in Sagittarius, you may find yourself ill at ease for no apparent reason. Simply tell yourself that it is the stars playing up, and, with any luck, this feeling will slowly begin to evaporate. Of course, if your conscience is bothering you, then the only person who can alter this state of affairs is your good self. Now for a look at the state of the Moon.

The Full Moon this month occurs in the sign of Sagittarius on 1 June. This is the area of your life which represents everything that is hidden from view. So, don't make any important moves at this time, because it is unlikely you are in possession of all the facts. Intuition could lead you astray too, so stick to your Capricorn common sense, and you will avoid any great difficulty.

The New Moon this month occurs in the airy sign of Gemini on 16 June. There is a suggestion here that either on this day or the day after there may be a minor new cycle occurring in connection with work. Certainly, if you have been feeling under par recently, the New Moon will have healing powers which will help you to get back to normal in record time. As always, New Moons can usefully be used for beginning anything new in all areas of life. Don't hesitate to use them, because they usually help to increase your confidence and feeling of well-being.

JULY

This is the time of the year when the Sun is in your opposite sign of Cancer and is trying to encourage you to be more co-operative in all your relationships. Those of you who work in professional partnerships or on behalf of other people, such as agent or manager, are sure to enjoy a prosperous period. For other Goats, it is time to ensure that you are giving and taking in equal amounts in that close personal relationship of yours. It is also a time when you may discover, to your horror, that somebody's ideas are better than your own. Never mind, Capricorn; you will get over the shock, and, besides, it is only a couple of weeks or so. And a couple of weeks during which you can learn quite a lot. The presence of Mars and Venus in Gemini certainly seem to be livening up your place of work, but there are certain dangers lurking here. Such a placing of the planet of emotion and sex seems to suggest that you will be strongly drawn to a member of the workforce, which, of course, is fine, if you happen to be fancy-free, but decidedly tricky if you are married. Still, there is no excuse for you, Capricorn, because you have one of the strongest wills under the zodiac, and nobody can force you into doing anything you don't want to do.

Financially, Uranus continues its retrograde movement through the cash area of life and, because of this, you must be your usual careful self. Cash matters can only be sorted out if you are prepared to confront them. Should you insist on hiding your head in the sand, the situation can only deteriorate. You have a heart as brave as any lion, and endurance, fortitude, determination to overcome difficulties, so all you need to do is face facts, and solutions will speedily present themselves to you.

This is a lucky time for those of you who work in the service industries or for other Goats who wish to hire the talents of other people, because you will be getting good value for money.

Socially, it is difficult to separate work from your private life, but my advice to you is, when entertaining colleagues, make sure that the special someone in your life is also invited. In this way you will be able to sidestep any potential temptation or embarrassing situation. Now for a look at the state of the Moon.

The Full Moon this month occurs in your own sign on the first of the month. Oh dear!, Just like Cancer, you can be strongly affected by this particular placing. So, if you wake up with a case of the 'grumbles' don't take yourself too seriously. Above all else, try to avoid allowing imagination to take flight, as you could very well become more insecure and lacking in confidence. After all, this is only a couple of days, and they will soon pass. In the meantime, avoid beginning anything new and sidestep important decisions.

The New Moon this month occurs in your opposite sign of Cancer, so it looks as if you will have the opportunity for meeting many new people. For some lucky Goats this could mean an important new romance. For others, circumstances are changing in an existing relationship.

This month we have what is known, as a Blue Moon, which means a second Full Moon in any given month. This particular one occurs in the airy sign of Aquarius, which happens to be the financial area of life. Now, during this period, you need to guard your possessions, because they could go missing or be mislaid, and you really don't want to spend hours looking down the back of sofas, under carpets, behind desks looking for prized possessions. It is also a time when a source of income may very well dry up; should this be the case, you need to start looking around quickly for an alternative. No matter how insecure or bad tempered you may feel during a Full Moon, you should try hard not to take out your mood on those closest to you. Go for a long walk or a swim, dispose of your stress in a physical way wherever possible. I leave it up to you to use your imagination.

AUGUST

Well, Capricorn, the position of the Sun in Leo for most of this month is certainly good news if you work in banks, big institutions or are perhaps an official or bureaucrat. For other Goats it is a great time for dealing with such people.

The presence of Venus and Mars in your opposite sign of Cancer is certainly throwing an optimistic and happy glow over emotional and sexual affairs. And, if you have decided to become engaged or married, you have been a very clever Goat indeed. Conversely, if you are fancy-free, it is just the time for meeting someone special, so get out your best outfit, shine up your shoes and circulate, because you don't want to miss out. A good time too for forming professional partnerships.

Right now, you even have a knack of being able to win over rivals and competitors. Yes, you have a silver tongue in your head. A great time then for forming professional partnerships. Your popularity is going through the ceiling, and there are many invitations and chances for you to have fun most of which you will be able to accept. Pluto has resumed direct movement, and that uneasy feeling you may have experienced over the last couple of months or so, slowly begins to disappear as you grow in self-esteem. Financially, you must continue to count all the small bills as well as the big ones.

Your ruling planet, Saturn, in retrograde movement in the area of your chart devoted to property and family, could cause some complications or at least delays in these areas. However because you are having such a good time in other life areas you may not even notice at the moment. August certainly looks to be an extremely promising and eventful period. Hopefully, you have managed to plan a short break or even a holiday. You couldn't have picked a better time if you have. Now for a look at the state of the Moon.

The New Moon this month occurs in the fiery sign of Leo on the 14th, an ideal time for facing up to responsibilities, the tax collector, those associated with insurance or even the bank manager. You can charm everybody on this day, so don't hesitate to plan something important, even if it does mean a confrontation.

The Full Moon occurs in the watery sign of Pisces on 28 August. It is a day to take care when you are out shopping, as bad purchases could be made. Your judgement is totally off when driving too, and if you can avoid a meeting or important discussion, so much the better, as you could say something at the wrong time to the wrong person in the wrong place. Aside from this, of course, the Full Moon always seem to undermine your self-esteem. Because of all this, stick to routine, and control adventurous impulses, for the time being anyway.

SEPTEMBER

Certainly, this particular month promises to be an interesting one, and on the working front it is exceptionally productive for Goats who are involved with foreign affairs, travel and educational pursuits in general. So, if you have decided to improve your mind and shake up your grey cells, this is the time for enrolling in some sort of course. Those of you who have loved ones abroad can be quite sure you will be hearing from them in the near future.

Other lucky professions are those connected with big money or large companies, such as insurance and banks. It is good for the Goat who needs to meet up with such people in order to, perhaps, sort out problems. Don't worry about this: be open and honest, and you will find they are much more prepared to make concessions than you had thought.

On a more personal level, for most of the month, there

will be occasions when you are wondering whether or not you wish to continue in a certain relationship. You are weighing the pros and cons of carrying on, but shouldn't rush in this direction. You want to make absolutely certain that you don't make a mistake.

Romantically, with Venus and Mars in Cancer during the first ten days of the month, there certainly is an interesting glow over the emotional and romantic side of life. If you are fancy-free, there is a great demand for your company, and you may find yourself hotly pursued by other people. If you want to be caught don't run too fast. If you happen to be in a steady relationship, this is a time for making commitments, getting engaged and walking up the aisle.

Professional relationships and partnerships formed during this month are sure to be lucky as well as profitable.

Financially, Uranus continues retrograde action for a little while longer, so you can't really relax in this area or take anything for granted. Should money be owed, see what you can do to rake it in.

Healthwise, the only real danger to you is perhaps a certain amount of stress caused by work or ambitions. Mercury continues to create a certain amount of minor confusions on the working front, and it is important that you keep these in proportion. Don't blow small matters out into major dramas. Providing you can do this then there should be minimum wear and tear on your nerves.

Where the family is concerned, it looks as if you may have to make an important decision on behalf of either a very young member of the family or an elderly one. Again, take your time; after all, that is the Capricorn way, and, by using this method, you won't make a mistake you will live to regret. Now let us have a look at the state of the Moon.

The New Moon this month occurs in the earthy sign of Virgo on the 12th, an ideal time for meeting new people, making contacts and also for long-distance travelling. Those of you who need to speed up a legal matter should not hesitate to do so at this time. But then again New Moons are always useful for tackling important matters in life.

The Full Moon during September occurs on the 27th in the fiery sign of Aries. This could make for minor changes within the family or a possibility of a lot of news and movement. Certainly, if you have decided to make changes or perhaps improve your surroundings, you couldn't have a better day. You may think this is going to be a quiet time, but people may descend upon you and the phone may never cease to ring. Somehow you acquire a certain quiet satisfaction from all of this activity. To add a little icing to the cake, this is also the day when Mercury decides to resume forward action. Therefore there are no pitfalls to worry about where documents, paperwork and travel are concerned. Keep the lines of communication wide open in all areas of life.

OCTOBER

During the first week of this month, the forward action of Mercury in the earthy sign of Virgo certainly seems to throw the emphasis on your ability to communicate far better than is usually the case. It is a great time for those in the media, the travel industry or people who need to express themselves on paper such as writers and members of the press. Mail that you are expecting from abroad, or maybe even special phone calls, come in on time which delight you.

From the 9th onwards this planet moves to the zenith of your chart and certainly gingers up your professional life. Because it is also joined by the Sun, there is a danger that you may spend too much time working. Well, this is the common Capricorn fault, isn't it? But, please try to remember, that there are other sides of life and people in it who want some of your time and attention. If you are not careful, you may find your popularity sinking together with a great deal of protestation from family or loved ones, who think they are being seriously neglected. Remember, life is about balance; it is certainly a good idea to work hard, but, in order to create an all-round healthy lifestyle, we need to relax and play as hard as we toil. Nevertheless, it is a good time for pushing forward with your ambitions as long as you keep your perspective.

Venus and Mars continue early month in the sign of Leo, so there could be some movement where big companies are concerned; certainly, if you are chasing them for money or perhaps getting together with them at meetings, you will be eloquent and able to put your point across without any difficulty at all.

From the 3rd onwards, Venus moves into Virgo, which is the area of your life devoted not only to education and improvement of the mind, but also travel. So, if you can wangle a weekend, or better still a couple of weeks away, this is an ideal time. Certainly, you will find romance, and your hotel and expectations will be fully met in all directions.

For those who are fancy-free, at home, there is a serious chance of your becoming involved with people who wouldn't normally attract you. They could come from completely different backgrounds for example, or possibly from abroad. Nevertheless, you are intrigued and infatuated. Better watch out if you are in a steady relationship or there could be trouble with a capital T.

Luckily, Neptune, who has been in retrograde action for quite some time, finally comes to its senses on the 6th. The confusion you may have been feeling on occasions slowly begins to evaporate. Those who work in creative jobs begin to make some startling progress.

Financially, because Uranus continues to be in retrograde movement, you must be vigilant where cash is concerned. Don't outlay unnecessarily large amounts of money, and ensure that you get good value. All in all October promises to be a reasonable month and, certainly, where ambitions are concerned there is a lot to be achieved, and you are just the person to make the most of these particular aspects. Now for a look at the state of the Moon.

The New Moon this month occurs in the airy sign of Libra on the 12th. This is, of course, the zenith of your chart. Therefore, you will be considering making certain changes where work or perhaps ambitions are concerned. Perhaps you are thinking about going off in a completely different direction. If so, providing you have done your homework, this will be a good idea. But, on no account do anything on impulse. When it comes to socializing during this period, there will be new faces, some of which will turn out to be useful contacts for the furtherance of your ambitions.

The Full Moon this month occurs in the earthy sign of Taurus on the 26th. This, generally speaking, is the fun area of life, because it stands for sports, partying, romance to a degree, and creative projects. Because we are still dealing with a Full Moon, there may be some confusion in one of these areas. Don't take anything for granted then; make sure you do your homework, and, if something should be delayed or cancelled, don't get yourself into a neurotic state.

Full Moons may not be the best news in the astrological scheme of things, but they are certainly useful if you want to clear out the dead wood from your life, and this is an appropriate time for doing just that. Mind you, if you are a parent, there may be one or two problems in connection with offspring, and you may be strongly tempted to reprimand them to extremes. Wait until the Full Moon has passed and you have managed to retain your sense of fair play, because, if you act at this time, you will make yourself unpopular with the entire family, and that will never do.

NOVEMBER

During November, the Sun and Mercury occupy the watery sign of Scorpio up until approximately mid-month. This throws the emphasis on teamwork and co-operation on a professional front. You may also be gaining a new objective or goal because of some advice you received. Contacts and friends will be all-important. They could be putting you on to a good thing, helping you to solve problems and genuinely encouraging you to let off a bit of steam and enjoy yourself. It is about time.

As far as work is concerned, Venus, at the zenith of your chart up until the 22nd, seems to make your load a great deal easier. You are getting on with workmates like a house on fire, and they are keen that you should join them socially as well as professionally. Now, you may not be too keen on this idea, but if you have a little rethink, I believe you will discover that this can be turned to your advantage, because there is a lot you can learn when other people are relaxed in their own homes that you could not possibly find out amid the hubbub of the office or the factory.

Romance may come to you through professional matters, so, if you are married, or in a steady relationship, you need to take care. When it comes to having fun, apart from mixing with friends, it would also be a good idea to visit clubs. Generally, you are an isolated creature, but, during this particular November, you want to get out and let off a lot of steam. Do this and it will certainly ease the stress you have been experiencing.

A word of warning. Mars squats in the sign of Virgo for the entire month; this could mean certain complications, stress and aggravation in connection with long-distance travelling. So, it is important that you visit strange lands; make sure you take your good manners with you and ensure that you are fully organized. If you are at home, you may be bumping into people who come from very different backgrounds and, though you may be curious about them, it won't pay for you to be too direct. Turn on that Capricorn charm; it is there somewhere; see if you can locate it.

Those of you who are attempting to improve your minds in the form of higher education should slow down your busy head. There is a tendency for you to be too impulsive and, because of this, mistakes can be made.

Cashwise, Uranus has finally resumed direct movement, and therefore money matters should begin to run a little more smoothly. Wouldn't you know it, just before Christmas, and it is necessary to start spending. Still, see what you can do to conserve and save before this becomes necessary.

Saturn continues in the home and property area of life. Unfortunately, it is in retrograde movement. So, because of this, there are likely to be some tensions between relatives and, I think it may be up to you to act the role of peacemaker. See what you can do to try and create a bit of harmony and goodwill. November seems to be full of promise with only one or two minor pitfalls

which you can surely overcome if you have a mind to
do so. Now for a look at the state of the Moon.

The New Moon this month occurs in the watery
sign of Scorpio on 11 November. This is the area of
your chart devoted to club activities, teamwork and
friendship. Clearly then, there is a new beginning in
connection with these areas of life perhaps fresh faces
and, if you are really lucky, even romance. As always
New Moons can be used effectively for furthering all
your secret wishes, so don't hesitate to dare just a little
more than is usually the case.

The Full Moon this month occurs on the 25th in the
airy sign of Gemini; this represents the working area
of life where things could get a little complicated, but
it also suggests that physically you may be running
downhill just a little. It might be a good idea to visit
the doctor or dentist if you are feeling off-colour, or set
aside periods for putting your feet up, resting, relaxing
and letting the whole world and all of its problems
just drift away. If you use this period in this fashion,
you will find that you will be revitalized, ready to get
back into life and continue your fight up the ladder of
success. A productive month.

DECEMBER

The practical side of your character loathes this time of
the year. So, you begin this month full of doom and
gloom, not to mention worry. Despite this, as the days
begin to fade away, you begin to catch the Christmas
spirit, a little like Scrooge in fact. Finally you splash
out and spoil everybody who is closest to you, and
by the time Christmas finally arrives, you are ready to
get in there, play the giddy Goat and thoroughly enjoy
yourself. Well, let's face it, if you have spent so much

money you might just as well have fun as sit around and moan about it.

The Sun's placing in Sagittarius up until the 21st reflects the rather quiet mood you are in at the beginning of the month. You can use this to your advantage, in order to catch up with jobs around the house or at work which have been left half done. Clear them away before the holiday starts. Remember, too, that physically you may be at a low ebb. You are after all approaching the end of your solar year, and it is only when you reach your birthday that you will begin to blossom once more. In the meantime do take care of yourself.

This is certainly a good month for a little bit of investigation, for rooting around behind the scenes. If your work is connected with such activities, you will be doing very well indeed. Try to use your intuitions and instincts rather than your active practical head, because they will serve you well during December. Venus' placing in Scorpio for the first couple of weeks seems to suggest that there will be loads of invitations for having fun and even romancing. Perhaps, in connection with your work or maybe in some hobby or pastime which involves teamwork or maybe clubs? Watch out, though, after this date because Venus goes into Sagittarius and you could play your own worst enemy where romance is concerned, becoming detrimentally involved with the opposite sex in some way. Perhaps you are already married and you are risking ruining your relationship with a harmless flirtation, or maybe it is the reverse that is true, and somebody else is perhaps not being completely honest with you. Quite frankly, Capricorn, you don't need this kind of aggravation; you can't cope with intrigue; it's just not in your nature. You invariably get caught out anyway.

Mars continues in Virgo, so those of you who are going away for the holidays really need to double check all arrangements, as confusion and general stress can be caused when on the move. But if you are your usual organized self, you should be able to sidestep this tiny pitfall.

Mercury enters your sign on the 5th, and you relax a little more. You become more adaptable to your surroundings, a little more like a chameleon, so that you can fit in almost with any kind of person and in any kind of scene. You are also more open-minded to unusual ideas on having fun, and are ready to do a little bit of party-going. Your mind is at its most efficient too, so, when it comes to work, you will be steaming through it in record time.

Luckily, Saturn has decided to resume direct movement just in time for Christmas, so, if you are spending time with the family there will be less complication than there would be otherwise. You need an excuse to put your feet up and relax, and Christmas provides this, of course. But, remember, if somebody else is doing all the hard graft, then it might be a good idea to volunteer to help out on occasions; otherwise your popularity could go through the floor.

Financially, you are your usual sensible self, except, of course, you can never resist spoiling yourself just once, while you are buying other people's presents, and why not, because you save for most of the year, and so why shouldn't you spoil yourself on occasions? I think that by the time this year is over you will realize that it has probably been one of the most successful for as long as you can remember, and that can't be a bad way to end any year. Now for a look at the state of the Moon.

The New Moon this month occurs in the fiery sign of Sagittarius. This, for you, will be boosting your intuition, your imagination, your ability to put yourself in somebody else's shoes, and problem solving will come second nature to you. You will also be more sensitive, so you need to spend your time with other people who are sympathetic to you, rather than those who antagonize or make you nervy.

The Full Moon occurs on the 24th in the sign of Cancer, so don't be at all surprised if somebody else close to you is rather stressed. If they are organizing Christmas, for heaven's sake lend a hand, try to keep them calm, cool and collected, otherwise you will start the festive period with a great deal of tension, and that is not the ideal way to begin the holidays. Avoid overindulgence because it may mean you will opt out of the preparations and your popularity will be in question if you do. Well, Capricorn, that is the end of another year and, as I have previously said, I think you will have now come to the conclusion that it has been a pretty kind one to you.

Daily Guide

JANUARY

MONDAY 1st The year begins with the Moon in Taurus so, quite clearly, although you may have had a hectic New Year's Eve you are prepared to carry on the celebrations for a little longer yet. What is more, Taurus is the area of your chart devoted to casual romance, too. So while others are nursing a sore head, you are rushing around looking for a little more action. If you are a family person, you will find that children are a sheer joy to spend time with, you will quite happily crawl around the floor playing with their recently purchased toys and generally trying to stimulate them. If you are fancy-free, sports may be at the top of your list of priorities and in this area you should find success.

TUESDAY 2nd Today, Mercury moves into Aquarius, the financial area of life, where it will stay for a few weeks. During this period there are sure to be occasions when you can gain from buying, selling, negotiating, attending meetings and also sorting out paperwork and, perhaps, for the lucky few signing an important financial document. Be prepared to find new ways of generating cash because that imagination of yours is firing on all cylinders, so don't waste it.

WEDNESDAY 3rd Today, as far as you are concerned,

is a red-letter day, because Jupiter has moved into your sign. This means that you can look forward to a year full of expansion, growth, lucky opportunities and more fun than you have experienced for quite some time. You will be far more carefree than the usual serious Goat. In fact, really quite 'giddy' on occasions. Nevertheless, this will be very attractive to other people, and social life is certainly going to be full of exciting opportunities to try new things and meet fresh faces.

THURSDAY 4th The Moon is in the airy sign of Gemini today and seems to be emphasizing the work side of life. Money and possessions are also very well-starred. But on a personal level the stars do warn you to try to keep a sense of proportion and not to take on too many new jobs or commitments. You are already overloaded. It is important you don't over extend yourself, otherwise you won't be able to enjoy the fruits of your hard labours.

FRIDAY 5th Today is the Full Moon and it occurs in your opposite sign of Cancer. Take care when dealing with other people at such a time as it is quite likely you will unintentionally give offence. If a relationship has been going through a rocky phase you may use this time for putting it out of its misery. If, on the other hand, you wish to save this particular bond then you will need to step up your efforts in order to try to put right that which has gone wrong. As always Full Moons can be used for bringing about the end of a job or a situation. Therefore they can be used positively.

SATURDAY 6th You are often shown to be ambitious and positively driven. There is a certain amount of truth in this, but you have a lot in common with your opposite sign of Cancer too, and you are much more emotional than you care to admit to others. Some time, during the next couple of days, you will have the chance to put yourself out for somebody else, a good deal less lucky than yourself. Do so, and don't count the cost.

SUNDAY 7th The Moon in Leo is pushing you to make your secret complaints known, and not fret too much about the impression you may create. There are so many planets now squatting in the cash area of your chart you must put your own interests first and do whatever is needed to protect what you won and earn.

MONDAY 8th Today, Mars moves into Leo, and from here on you will be well advised to do your best not to antagonize those in positions of power or authority, officialdom or even bureaucrats. Should it become necessary to discuss your financial state with them, do your best to be helpful and above all else polite. This doesn't mean crawling to them, but neither should you become too abrasive, though you will be strongly tempted to do so.

TUESDAY 9th Today, Mercury moves into retrograde action, and this state of affairs will exist until the 30th. In the meantime it is best, wherever possible to avoid dealing with important paperwork and certainly side-step signing important documents. Should it become necessary for you to travel for any reason at all then double check all your arrangements as muddle and confusion are likely to reign during this period.

WEDNESDAY 10th With the Moon in the earthy sign of Virgo today the emphasis seems to be on improving your mind or perhaps, physically getting out and about as much as possible. You are certainly in an adventurous mood. Also if you are waiting to hear from somebody you care about, who lives some way from you, you can be quite sure they will not let you down. This evening be even more adventurous; try a new hobby or leisure-time activity.

THURSDAY 11th Mars cosies up with Pluto today and this will certainly be energizing team effort and the lives of your friends. They may be coming to you for advice because they know how strong, dependable and reliable you are. This isn't to say that they think you are at all boring, but at least it is always nice to know a Capricorn is there when the rest of us are falling apart.

FRIDAY 12th This is the day when your money planet, Uranus, finally enters the cash area of your chart, where it will remain for the rest of the year. This should certainly improve your chances of swelling the bank balance and opportunities to do so are likely to come in from unusual people or completely out of the blue. You need to rethink your attitude to the materialistic side of life and be prepared to consider practically anything.

SATURDAY 13th Mercury is in a beautiful aspect with Mars today. This certainly seems to be livening up the family, and also your home life. Possibly you are considering entertaining this evening, and if so you couldn't have picked a better time. You have a chance, too, to sit down and sensibly discuss differences with relatives without anybody flying off the handle. Try not to make it too late a night as energy may run out later on.

SUNDAY 14th In many ways your sign is the luckiest and most protected in the zodiac right now due to the fact that Jupiter is squatting in your sign. Other aspects are encouraging you to risk everything in search of the security and success you know you richly deserve. Anything romantic or creative begun now will have the mark of success written all over it. Make the most of this day as you will surely regret it if you fail to do so.

MONDAY 15th That planet of creativity, love, peace and harmony, Venus enters the sign of Pisces. This will certainly help to improve your relationship with brothers and sisters, and also will be making you feel much more optimistic. On a romantic level, brief encounters seem a possibility and just for once you won't fight temptation but decide to give in gracefully. All sounds a bit difficult if you happen to be married.

TUESDAY 16th A wonderful aspect between the Sun and Neptune today. It is certainly good news for those of you who are studying or perhaps the Goat who wishes to make a few changes either to surroundings or image. Time to be more experimental then. This will work wonders in your love life, and, particularly if you are fancy-free, you will find yourself in great demand.

WEDNESDAY 17th Retrograde Mercury has now moved back into your sign, and in the next couple of days you need to be very careful of what you commit to writing and any commitments or promises you make verbally to other people, because you may have the tendency to promise more than you can comfortably come up with when the time is necessary.

THURSDAY 18th A beautiful aspect between the Sun and Mercury today seems to suggest that your mind will be put at ease where an official matter is concerned. It is a great time for travelling; and for greater communication with other people whether it be over the telephone or in deep discussion. Time then to sort out differences between yourself and those who really matter in your life.

FRIDAY 19th As a rule you stick like glue to your opinions but admire others who stand up for their own convictions. Now that the Moon has entered your sign you could easily find yourself drawn to someone whose way of life is directly at odds with your own. This may surprise some, but the truth is that you are more forgiving and thoughtful than you usually admit.

SATURDAY 20th Today is the day of the New Moon, and it occurs in your sign. Therefore you are the most popular person in the zodiac at the moment. Make sure you keep a very high profile and go after whatever or whoever it is you want out of life. A good time, too, for making minor changes, and a new cycle could be starting in your life in some areas.

SUNDAY 21st The Sun is in a beautiful aspect with your money planet Uranus today. On the one hand, it may result in somebody repaying a loan you had long forgotten, on the other, it could be that a bout of extravagance overtakes you. Nevertheless, you will still be on the search for value for money. Either way it promises to be an interesting day.

MONDAY 22nd The Sun is now firmly entrenched in the money area of your chart and that is where the emphasis will stay for approximately a month. During this period you will be unwilling to do anything for anybody unless you are recompensed in the appropriate fashion. You will also be saving more perhaps, with a special item you want to buy, or maybe a summer holiday in mind. Whatever the reason, heaven help anyone attempting to part you from your money. Door-to-door salesmen receive short shrift.

TUESDAY 23rd Today, the stars will be providing you with a tremendous amount of vitality and increasing your determination to get things done despite rivals or opposition. There is a chance though that occasionally you may leave an unfortunate impression that you are being a little too domineering. But, the stars will help you to achieve your heart's desire and workmates and bosses will be impressed by your efforts.

WEDNESDAY 24th Today, there may be some temporary difficulties in your intense personal life. However, the stars also suggest that a little sympathy and patience will now help you to avoid a great deal of hurt at a later date. Bear in mind, too, that you could certainly benefit from resting up this evening.

THURSDAY 25th The aspects seem to be a bit of a mix today. Because of this, you must expect a certain amount of misunderstanding or disagreement. Conversely, one aspect suggests that if you have not yet managed to free yourself from a suffocating relationship, now is the time to make a dash for the door. Be careful though, that in doing so you don't leap from one bad relationship into another.

FRIDAY 26th You are in an optimistic mood for a change and because you are expecting something to turn up it is likely that it will, this is the power of positive thinking in operation. Even so, you can't afford to wait for things to happen, otherwise you are liable to miss out on something important. Family matters especially need your immediate attention. Sadly you can't afford to believe that everyone has your best interests at heart.

SATURDAY 27th This is one of those days when the more you give, the more others will expect. So, at some point you are really going to have to put your foot down. The main difficulty appears to be that you have been so supportive in the past, that others, including the family, automatically assume you will be there for them all the time. You have no alternative but to put them straight, and while doing so, create more time for what you really want to do with your life.

SUNDAY 28th Today, it is very much a case of the more you are challenged the keener you will be to respond. In fact, you can now go a long way towards disproving the unflattering theory that you are too depressed to bother to do much with your life. You have wider concerns and a more interesting view than most, but when it comes to exploiting a proper chance you are quick off the mark.

MONDAY 29th Right now, the Moon in Mercury suggests that much depends on how you express yourself, your feelings and your opinions in particular, whether or not you can keep the more ambitious or critical side of your nature under strict control. You are right to expect both respect and help, but on no account, should you dramatize your intense personal life or even your cash difficulties. Otherwise other people are quite likely to put even more restrictions in your way, and you don't need this.

TUESDAY 30th This is the day when Mercury finally resumes forward movement; you will now feel it much easier to communicate with other people, travelling will be less fraught and, should you decide to turn your attention to paperwork, you will be speeding through it at a rate of knots, leaving others positively amazed. A good time too for making minor changes.

WEDNESDAY 31st The Moon in Gemini could leave you feeling a little flat or exhausted on this the last day of the month. If this should prove to be the case, then pace yourself or even take a couple of hours off in order to rest up. This advice applies particularly if you have something special planned for this evening, whether it be of a romantic or social nature.

FEBRUARY

THURSDAY 1st The Moon is in your opposite sign today, and it is necessary for you to consider the wants and needs of other people as well as your own. There are times when you become so wrapped up in yourself and your achievements that you can neglect those closest to you. Today, this simply won't do Capricorn, so show everybody the softer side of your character.

FRIDAY 2nd Venus is in a beautiful aspect with your ruling planet, Saturn. This makes you more sociable, romantic and also creative. Try in some way to make this day a special day, either for yourself or for other people. If you are fancy-free, you could very well be temporarily infatuated with someone and, as long as you don't take the relationship too seriously, you could have the time of your life. Lots to look forward to then.

SATURDAY 3rd It will certainly be a rare Goat who doesn't take advantage of all the planetary activity that is going on in your sign at the moment. You will be paying attention to your long-term ambitions and may slowly be changing your habits or your methods. You are also likely to be much more adaptable, so go where your instincts take you, even if it means leaving the path behind and starting again from square one.

SUNDAY 4th The Full Moon today in Leo strongly suggests that you obey all traffic rules and regulations. If you try to get away with anything then I am afraid you are likely to get caught, under the influence of this particular Moon.

MONDAY 5th Although your competitive instincts are certainly firing on all cylinders, there are a number of sound reasons why you must take a softer, more sympathetic approach to emotional and professional relationships. Even the most hardbitten of Goats will find today that aggression simply won't work. Harmony, co-operation and no confrontation should be your motto.

TUESDAY 6th The Moon in the earthy sign of Virgo is certainly encouraging you to be a little more adventurous. Apply different methods to routine jobs. Visit places in your spare time that you have never been to before. A time for throwing off the old and taking on the new, and that includes relationships too. So, if someone is behaving completely out of order it may be time to abandon them completely.

WEDNESDAY 7th It is time to step back from what you are planning or arranging and make certain that your plans and your dreams are based in reality. The aspects today could do wonders for your powers, intuition and imagination. But, unless you control your enthusiasm and mix it with a clear understanding of your own limits, your losses could easily outweigh your gains. It is up to you.

THURSDAY 8th It looks as if you are about to enter an important phase for relationship and partnership matters. However, you still need to sort out certain cash and family problems before you can turn your attention to your emotional life. Luckily, an aspect today suggests that a breakthrough is over the horizon, even though other people, including loved ones, still seem determined to make your life as difficult as possible.

FRIDAY 9th That planet of harmony and romance moves into the sign of Aries which for you rules the family and property areas of life. During the next few days, you could develop the urge to spend on your surroundings, to brighten them up which seems to be a reflection of the more optimistic mood you feel, yourself, and want to see reflected all around you. Problems with family begin to fade away in the next couple of weeks or so, and home entertaining will be extremely enjoyable.

SATURDAY 10th During the morning, you find it extremely difficult to turn focus away from ambitions and give your full attention to your social life or people you have made social arrangements with. Luckily, during the afternoon your mood changes and you become light-hearted and a sheer delight to spend time with. Team sports are especially well-starred.

SUNDAY 11th Venus is in a beautiful aspect with Pluto today and it looks as if those friends of yours will have some wonderful ideas on how you can spend your leisure-time in a more exciting way. Romance too is rather prone to change. Someone you were once strongly attracted to is suddenly viewed as though they were one of Frankenstein's monsters. This is probably because you have found somebody fresh to tempt you away.

MONDAY 12th You must remember today that any worthwhile task or job is also one which is worth being paid for, so make a fuss if you believe you are still receiving less than you truly deserve. The aspects today are likely to show you a series of alternatives; all you need is the bravery to change direction and let fate be your guide.

TUESDAY 13th The Moon in Sagittarius puts you in a thoughtful mood. Just for once you should force yourself to rely on your instinct and hunches rather than your practical, down-to-earth brain. You are certain there aren't many problems which cannot be solved with sheer common sense, particularly when it comes to feelings, both your own and other people's.

WEDNESDAY 14th Mars moves into the sign of Pisces, and this will certainly be keeping you on the go over the next few weeks or so. But there will be a tendency for you to be a little too impulsive when driving, and this needs conscious controlling. On a personal level, there may be many brief encounters but they are likely to be mere physical attraction rather than anything more serious.

THURSDAY 15th Mercury moves into the money area of life which is interesting because it seems to suggest you can gain through travelling, paperwork, or legal matters. If you are short of cash then these are the areas where you should be concentrating most of your energies. Minor changes to your attitude will also help your cause.

FRIDAY 16th Mercury is in a beautiful aspect with your money planet, Uranus, today. So, if money is owed don't think twice before communicating your displeasure to other people either in writing or on the telephone. For many that proverbial 'cheque in the post' finally arrives, much to your delight. Make sure that you don't spend it in celebration this evening.

SATURDAY 17th Mercury is in a fine aspect with Pluto today, and many changes and lots of news seem to be arriving in connection with your friendship circle. Whatever you do, though, don't hand on gossip or repercussions will be felt for some considerable while. New people you meet today will become firm friends almost over night. A good time too for team sports.

SUNDAY 18th The New Moon today falls in the financial area of life, but because this is a Sunday it might be rather difficult to gain in any way, so use the time for making financial plans which you can implement tomorrow, when a fresh source of income may pop up and introduce itself.

MONDAY 19th Mars is in an explosive mood with Pluto today, and if I were you, I would give friends and acquaintances a wide berth because they are rash, impetuous, impatient and bad tempered. Fortunately, you are an independent soul and can struggle on for twenty-four hours unaided, without any difficulty whatsoever.

TUESDAY 20th Today the Sun is firmly entrenched in

the sign of Pisces; good news for those of you who work in the media, travelling or sales, or the Goat who wishes to go to interviews, negotiations or meetings of any description. You will find the power to communicate your thoughts and feelings a good deal easier over the next few weeks.

WEDNESDAY 21st No doubt you don't want to be reminded that you may have made a few financial mistakes in the past. Nevertheless, this is the day for putting joint arrangements on a much more concrete footing. One way or another you have been a little careless recently and now you have no choice but to stick to your budget and avoid non-essentials. Other people know exactly what is expected of them in all areas, so at least you don't have to worry about that.

THURSDAY 22nd The Sun is at odds with Pluto today and you may find acquaintances and friends are just that little too bossy, cocky or overconfident. Think twice though before telling them the way you feel; in fact the best thing to do is to act independently and leave them to their own devices. In this way you will avoid any bad feeling.

FRIDAY 23rd Situations which have recently left you feeling somewhat confused should now pose no problem whatsoever. In fact, others will be falling over themselves to help you out and push you in the right direction. You seem to have the backing and support of the right people and you will certainly not be short of chances to make use of them.

SATURDAY 24th The Moon in the earthy sign of Taurus promises good times ahead. The emphasis is on creativity, and you will certainly be offered every chance to show what you are really made of. The stars will help to bring your artistic talents into the spotlight, and you may even get the opportunity to turn a spare time hobby into something more profitable. A person with eccentric ideas is about to bring luck into your life.

SUNDAY 25th There is so much activity on your chart at this time, particularly where your social and professional life is concerned; the sole danger seems to be that you may be trying to spread your efforts a little too much. So, the thing to do is be more selective, and patient, and it won't be long before you find the success and recognition you need.

MONDAY 26th Today your morale and self-confidence seem to be soaring, but this doesn't mean you can afford to take situations or people for granted. Certainly, some kind of progress can be made, but there is also the possibility that it will have to be paid for in the near future if you are not careful.

TUESDAY 27th The Moon in Gemini suggests minor changes going on in the lives of your workmates and also at work. The thing to do right now is to be as adaptable as possible and not to question too much the wisdom of superiors. This evening you need to get out and let off a bit of steam; try to do so with people with whom you have a great deal in common.

WEDNESDAY 28th Creatively and romantically you should be in your element at the moment, but you won't be able to relax completely until a long-standing family dispute has been solved to everybody's satisfaction. With the Moon in Cancer today it is very likely that changes are taking place in an existing relationship.

If you are fancy-free someone new will be entering your scene.

THURSDAY 29th There may be a strong temptation today to jump to conclusions, and if you do you will quickly discover that your imagination has been playing tricks on you. This in turn could lead to an unnecessary separation if you say or do the wrong thing. Be your usual cautious self then, and the month won't end on a low note.

MARCH

FRIDAY 1st The Sun is in a beautiful aspect with sexy, passionate and aggressive Mars today. Because of this, you will have added vitality and sex appeal, and should push ahead with whatever is important to you, particularly in your intense personal life. If you are a freelance worker, you will have sufficient nerve to approach those who would normally intimidate you. Very much a case then today of 'he who dares wins'.

SATURDAY 2nd The Moon in Leo seems to suggest that you are in a good mood and determined to look to the future. But don't be in so much of a hurry to change things that you unwittingly dispose of something which might prove useful at a later date. If you can bring yourself to shift your sights slightly, and try to see things differently, you will meet with great success.

SUNDAY 3rd Those closest to you, at work, in the family and in your romantic life, are in a flamboyant, enthusiastic and go-getting mood. There is no point in going into competition with them, you may just as well resign yourself to the fact that it is necessary to take a back seat and allow them to step into the limelight. If you do this, then harmony will be maintained.

MONDAY 4th The Moon in Virgo could put you in a day-dreamy kind of mood, and, because of this, it would be a bad idea to turn your attention to anything which requires a great deal of concentration or detailed work. Stick to routine and plan something special for this evening. If you have romance in mind, this could be the explanation for your current mood. Certainly the evening seems to find you at your most popular, and if you are fancy-free it shouldn't be difficult to find someone who can appreciate your finer points.

TUESDAY 5th The Full Moon today occurs in the sign of Virgo. Not a time then for being too adventurous, and any opportunities which come to you through new faces should be seriously investigated before commitment. And even then, you must wait until the Full Moon period has passed in order to avoid possible miscalculations or bad judgement. Those of you waiting on calls or letters from abroad are likely to be disappointed at this time.

WEDNESDAY 6th That planet of the arts, creativity and love, namely Venus, moves into the sign of Taurus today, the area of your life devoted to fun, amusement, children and romance. There is clearly going to be a rosy glow over these matters over the next few weeks. However, it is unlikely that you will be serious, for an uncharacteristic, flirty mood descends. Despite this, there are plenty of chances for fun and party-going and you will be in just the mood to take advantage of the fact. A light-hearted fun time lies ahead. Be optimistic.

THURSDAY 7th   That planet of communication, Mercury moves into the sign of Pisces, which is also the area of your chart devoted to movement, change and your thought pattern. Because Pisces is renowned for its indecisiveness, you could go through a couple of weeks when it is much more difficult than is usually the case to make up your mind. This is for the best possible reason. It seems you are anxious to ensure that you do the right thing, at the right time, for the right person.

FRIDAY 8th   The Sun is in a wonderful aspect with Mercury today, and you will want to keep on the move as much as possible. Should you be confined or restricted in your environment for any reason whatsoever, you will become bored quickly and rather snappy. Cram much activity into the day, and see as many people as possible.

SATURDAY 9th   Mercury is in a challenging aspect with Pluto today and, because of this, you will find it more than usually difficult to make up your mind. Just as you come down on one side of a situation or a problem you suddenly realize the benefits of the other point of view. Wherever possible then, the best thing to do is to shelve committing yourself for the time being and turn your attention to routine matters around the home, or simply to pleasure-seeking. Why not?

SUNDAY 10th   Friends seem anxious for your company at the moment, and there is certainly plenty of news and gossip going the rounds. But remember, Capricorn, you do like a good scandal, and can be easily led into passing on confidences. If you do this, you will find yourself in hot water, right up to your neck, at a later date. So honour confidences above all else.

MONDAY 11th Whatever has happened in the past, it might be a good idea to reveal it now while other people are in the mood to forgive and forget. The stars today hold out the promise of a new beginning, once you have been completely honest about what you have done and what you still intend to do. Far from reacting negatively other people are likely to be suitably impressed, maybe even inspired by your honesty.

TUESDAY 12th This is one of those occasions when even the most reserved Goat can make a bold move and act completely out of character. Certain aspects today put you in a dynamic mood, so that even those who thought they knew you well are about to be amazed by just how adventurous you have become. Best of all this is a constructive time which will last for some while.

WEDNESDAY 13th The Moon is in your sign making you a little indecisive, but the more you delay making decisions over domestic or cash matters, the more it will haunt you. Even if you manage to ignore your conscience, you won't be able to ignore other people's reminders that you simply don't have much more time. The planets are urging you to be braver and more confident, even though deep down you probably feel anything but.

THURSDAY 14th Today it may appear to you as if others are trying to leave you out in some way. But you will only make matters worse if you let them see what they are doing is having any kind of effect on you at all. So, show indifference right now, even though you may be longing to know what is happening. Because the more you push for answers, the less you will be told.

FRIDAY 15th Even if you are one of those Goats who

doesn't consider themselves to be a typical Capricorn, today certain aspects are sure to bring out the competitive, ambitious side of your character. You are certainly in no mood to suffer fools gladly, in fact others will soon realize you are determined to have your own way and, if they have any common sense whatsoever, they won't try to stop you.

SATURDAY 16th For some time now you have had the feeling that your daily routine needs to be transformed or changed; you certainly appear to be putting in a great deal of effort for precious little reward. Luckily, today suggests a new beginning, an opportunity or a chance to scrap whatever is outmoded and useless, and start again. Consider anything which makes your workload easier.

SUNDAY 17th The Sun cosies up to your ruling planet, Saturn, today, and you are flooded with solar power: warm, friendly, confident and as ready as you are ever going to be to get whoever, or whatever you want out of this life. If you have been pacing around waiting for the right time to make a romantic move, well believe you me this is it – get cracking.

MONDAY 18th The Moon in Pisces finds you shilly-shallying over fiddly little details when you should be decisive over major ones. You will find it hard to sit still and, because of this, it might be a good idea to forget about work, which requires a great deal of concentration, for the time being. This evening you need to keep on the go in order to burn up some of that nervous energy.

TUESDAY 19th The New Moon today falls in the sign of Pisces bringing with it added inspiration, more mental flexibility and the chance of meeting new and interesting people. Should you be a freelance worker, this is an ideal time for pushing ahead for that special assignment you have had your eye on. News from a brother or sister is also a likely possibility.

WEDNESDAY 20th The Sun changes signs now and moves into the fiery sign of Aries. This is the area of your chart devoted to family, home and property. So, problems or complications in this area can now be sorted out with greater aplomb. You are also likely to find yourself entertaining on your own base far more than is usually the case, and thoroughly enjoying the experience. Problems with relatives are easily solved.

THURSDAY 21st Mars is in a beautiful aspect with your ruling aspect, Saturn. This certainly floods you with extra vitality and sex appeal, and encourages the passionate side of your nature which you generally prefer to hide. You could find yourself getting into heated arguments, but you may also find that you are exceptionally attractive to the opposite sex who will be giving chase in a big way. Don't run too fast.

FRIDAY 22nd Anything of a romantic nature should turn out for the best if you play your astrological cards right. Creative activities are well-starred too, although if you want them to last, you must at least try to take other people's wishes and needs into consideration. Be warned though, that whatever you start right now you will be expected to finish. So select your ambitions or objectives with a bit of caution.

SATURDAY 23rd The Sun is in a sparkling aspect with Pluto today and certainly friends are in top form. They will be popping in and livening up your day just when you had thought it was going to be boring. If you feel like visiting a club then do so, because that is where you can find romance if you happen to be fancy-free. So give it a whirl.

SUNDAY 24th   Mercury moves into the fiery sign of Aries bringing about minor changes and a considerable amount of movement on the home front during the next few weeks or so. Those of you who are hoping to find somewhere new to live should strike gold during the next couple of weeks and will be signing on the dotted line. Others, who want to make changes in a family, shouldn't hesitate.

MONDAY 25th   Mars now joins Mercury in the sign of Aries and this certainly steps up the action on the home front. Mind you, it will be all too easy for you to get into disagreements and arguments with other people without really understanding how they started off in the first place. Somebody has got to keep their temper, and as you are a well-controlled Goat it might just as well be you.

TUESDAY 26th   At some point today the Moon will be moving into your opposite sign of Cancer bringing in a great deal of change in the lives of those who mean the most to you. If you are fancy-free it is certainly a time for getting out and about because your chances of meeting new people are very strong, don't then sit at home complaining about being lonely. Do something positive about it.

WEDNESDAY 27th   Mars is in a wonderful aspect with Pluto today, and if you are considering asking friends round for a small party or perhaps a meal, then you couldn't have picked a better day. The company will be uplifting and sparkling and their ideas will set your own imagination on fire. A good time too for important discussions with relatives.

THURSDAY 28th The Sun is in a beautiful aspect with Mercury today, a time when you will find it much easier to express how you really feel, on the emotional level and also mentally. Don't be afraid to present your ideas to other people at work, because they are going to be well received contrary to the reaction you were expecting. Those who are travelling should enjoy a profitable as well as enjoyable day.

FRIDAY 29th It is fair to say that all Goats are not necessarily as domineering as others. In fact, all Capricorns are advised to take a much softer line in all relationships both professional and personal. Over the next couple of weeks or so you won't get a better chance to learn the benefits of co-operation, harmony and even partnerships.

SATURDAY 30th If you need some kind of help from a more experienced or superior person on a social or professional level, then this is the time to ask for it. Someone you have found difficult to approach lately is now only too keen to pass on the benefits of their experience to you. Naturally, some of their ideas are bound to seem a little old hat at first, but eventually they will be a source of inspiration and success to you.

SUNDAY 31st There is a good chance that you may be in two minds about which way to move, where important marital or romantic affairs are concerned. However, some kind of decision is needed, and if you don't make it now, someone else might just take the initiative, with results not to your liking. So push ahead regardless of injured pride. Remember, the honest approach is the best one.

APRIL

MONDAY 1st What a lovely start to the month: a fabulous aspect between Venus and Neptune throws a sentimental and romantic veil over the day. Naturally, this probably won't benefit you on a professional level but, when it comes to romance or having fun, this evening you are in a highly receptive mood and easily charmed by the opposite sex. If you are in a relationship, make this a special evening in some way.

TUESDAY 2nd There really isn't any point in being subtle today because flattery is the way you should go; it will get you everywhere. In fact, this is the right time to put your schemes and plans to one side, come right out and ask for exactly what you want. But be warned, adopt a softer approach, particularly where family or relationship affairs are concerned, even where you secretly believe certain people just don't deserve it.

WEDNESDAY 3rd The Moon in Libra today squats at the zenith of your chart suggesting minor changes in connection with ambitions. You may have thought yourself 'set fair' for an easy course, but now you begin to wonder at the wisdom of your decision. However, although it may be a good idea to reconsider, it is important you don't shilly-shally too long, or opportunity may pass you by and visit somebody else.

THURSDAY 4th Today is the day of the Full Moon, and it occurs in the sign of Libra. Avoid making decisions in connection with work and ambitions because it is likely that you are unaware of all the true facts. They may emerge at a later date, and put you in an embarrassing position if you act right now. Very much a time then for adopting a policy of 'wait and see'.

FRIDAY 5th Venus moves into Gemini today, and this should improve the health of those of you who have been several degrees under. However, it is also a placing which encourages excesses. Too many sweet things or alcohol may take their toll although it has to be admitted that you may decide you are quite happy to pay the price for these indulgences. The choice is up to you.

SATURDAY 6th The Sun is in a challenging aspect with Jupiter today, and this could lead you into being overconfident about a situation or relationship. On the working front you may be a little careless too, but you must remember that the stars impel; they do not compel. You are the master or mistress of your own fate, and can control this tendency if you have a mind to.

SUNDAY 7th Your ruling planet, Saturn, moves into the fiery sign of Aries today where it will stay for approximately two years. During this period you may gather some extra responsibility; it may come in the wonderful form of an addition to the family, or perhaps increased expenditure. Either way you have the strength to overcome and far more enterprising enthusiasm at your fingertips than you have had for many moons.

MONDAY 8th Today, Mercury moves into the fun area of your life, namely into the sign of Taurus. Strangely enough, although there will be chances to go out and enjoy yourself, you may become fascinated by such hobbies as backgammon, collecting books or maybe even chess. Possibly somebody you admire greatly is interested in such things and you are trying to go out of your way to please them.

TUESDAY 9th Because there is a Moon in your sign today, you should be feeling much more vital and confident about the result of recent talks or negotiations. Furthermore, you have just enough time to regain control of certain major areas of your life in which at present others seem to be lauding it up. Perhaps it is time to make your presence felt?

WEDNESDAY 10th Do try hard to drag your thoughts away from set-backs and refuse to be bullied or waste any more time on self-pity. Whether you choose to make yourself miserable, or happy, the amount of effort it needs is exactly the same. You have a great deal going for you at present, and plenty of energy at your disposal – don't waste it on focusing on things that went wrong rather than the many good things which have happened to you recently.

THURSDAY 11th Someone may describe you as being too materialistic, but let's face it we all have to pay the bill. Also when the pressure is on, you can be a lot more resourceful and determined than most give you credit for. Luckily, you won't have to push too hard over the next few days because the stars suggest your luck, personally as well as financially, will be taking a turn for the better.

FRIDAY 12th A bit of gossip you hear by way of somebody else may cause you to doubt your senses, or at the very least question the wisdom of a decision recently made. But there is still a great deal going on that you can't possibly know about, so don't try to back out of a promise just yet. Also, bear in mind that there really isn't any need for you to be quite so cautious, or to make any unnecessary apologies.

SATURDAY 13th It probably won't come as a surprise to you if those you are trying to get on your side reject your attempts completely, but don't make a fuss, and certainly don't take it personally, because this is not the end of the affair by any means. In fact, in the very near future, roles could be reversed and other people might just begin to start chasing you, which will be rather nice.

SUNDAY 14th Today you must take every chance to express yourself and explain why you have chosen to follow certain paths. Those you have to deal with on a regular basis may not always agree with you, but at least they will begin to understand what you are trying to achieve.

MONDAY 15th Mars is in a challenging aspect with Jupiter today and opportunities, which seem to be good and hold the promise of a great deal of profit, may not be all they seem. Therefore look into them. Avoid too, taking the advice of relatives because their judgement is as clouded as your own.

TUESDAY 16th Although you seem to know exactly what you want and have no doubt that you will get it, you will have to take other people's views and suggestions into account if you are to make good progress. It looks as if the time has finally arrived for you to be less demanding, and perhaps to take on a more sensible approach to fulfilling your long-term ambitions.

WEDNESDAY 17th The New Moon in the fiery sign of Virgo is likely to suggest a fresh cycle in connection with property or family, you may hear news of a wedding or birth, or maybe somebody has decided to throw an impromptu party. If you are on the look out for the ideal home you may just find it today.

THURSDAY 18th Mercury is in a beautiful aspect with Jupiter today. This puts you in a buoyant mood and physically you are in top form with a shiny coat and a suitably wet nose. Workmates seem to be clamouring round you to join in on a social occasion; one of them may even make an interesting introduction which could eventually lead to romance.

FRIDAY 19th You are in a really good mood and ready to make some gigantic strides in all the important areas of your life. Despite this you may be faced with a difficult decision. Make it, then forget about it, because you have far too much going for you to waste time wondering about what might have been. Generally, you must act rather than talk, even though others will be watching whatever you do.

SATURDAY 20th The Sun moves into the earthy sign of Taurus today and this, of course, represents the fun area of life as well as matters related to children. It looks as if you are more prepared to turn your attention to having fun, party-going, sports and romance. A light-hearted Goat is a giddy Goat, and this in turn generally means that you are the life and soul of any gathering you decide to attend. Those in artistic jobs will be doing exceptionally well.

SUNDAY 21st It is unlikely that you will be able to sit still for a moment today, and even more unlikely that you won't meet up with some kind of change along the way. Aspects today suggest that you are still searching for something, and seem to believe that the further or faster you travel, the more likely you are to find it. Wrong! The answers you want are literally under your nose – if only you would start asking the right questions.

MONDAY 22nd Your self-control is admirable and you usually pride yourself on your ability to stay serene, even in the face of the most difficult circumstances. But, even the Goat needs to erupt occasionally, and today sudden changes suggest that your patience is about to give way. Some harsh words will be spoken but at least you will be doing most of the talking.

TUESDAY 23rd Of course, as you no doubt know, life tends to go in circles, and sooner or later the old must give way to the new. It is likely that the stars today will bring you face to face with people who see things in a totally different way from yourself. Remember it is how you deal with differences and disagreements that would determine how the rest of the year develops. Whether those you have trusted in the past can be relied upon in the future may be in doubt.

WEDNESDAY 24th New and interesting people are likely to enter your life today, either at work or in your social life this evening. Be alert though, because at least one of them may be able to help your ambitions come true, and still another offers you the opportunity for an unforgettable romantic experience. So, no skulking at home today.

THURSDAY 25th The Moon in Leo brings in some

unwanted news from an official source, and you are likely to blow this out of all proportion. Instead of panicking, get some advice from a wiser or more experienced head because this will help put your mind at ease. Once you know the full facts you will be able to relax, rather than driving yourself into a nervous breakdown. Make sure you get out this evening, you certainly will need to rest those jangling nerves.

FRIDAY 26th It is likely that you are beginning to wonder whether the efforts you are making on behalf of somebody else are really worthwhile, because you are getting very little in the way of encouragement, praise, or even thanks. It seems that you are being completely taken for granted, and the only way to alter this situation is to stand up for yourself in no uncertain fashion.

SATURDAY 27th You are a little hypersensitive today and, because of this, must not take any kind of criticism too seriously because it is meant kindly. If you want to be really safe and sure, spend your time with old friends rather than new, because they will know exactly how to handle you. If you are in need of a day for simply resting up and doing what you please, then this is it. Make a few calls this evening, though, as loneliness could seep through at this time.

SUNDAY 28th A beautiful aspect from Pluto with your ruling planet, Saturn, suggests that circumstances around you are changing for the better. You are certainly beginning to feel a bit more optimistic, mainly due to the support and encouragement you are receiving from your closest friends. If you are taking part in any kind of sport today it should be successful. Clubs are also worth visiting.

MONDAY 29th Mercury is in a beautiful aspect with Neptune today, and you may find it difficult to concentrate on any job. Your mind keeps drifting off into the past. Possibly there is a reason for this, perhaps a special occasion which needs celebrating or maybe you bumped into an old friend you haven't seen for simply years. However pay extra attention when dealing with paperwork for fear of making mistakes.

TUESDAY 30th Neptune moves into retrograde movement on this, the last day of the month, so you may be experiencing some difficulties or problems in connection with a brother or a sister. Certainly, any short trips that you take need to be well planned as even the most simple journey can become unbelievably difficult and arduous. Never mind, now you know, you can do all you can to offset this aspect.

MAY

WEDNESDAY 1st The Sun, in a beautiful aspect with Neptune, will increase your sensitivities. You will be drawn to harmonious surroundings, peaceful people and colourful settings. Pace yourself throughout the day. There is no need to rush around, you will achieve just as much by taking things at a slightly slower pace, and then you will have plenty of energy left for this evening when somebody may be quite demanding on the emotional or physical level.

THURSDAY 2nd Plenty of news arrives in connection with friends, thanks to the fact that the Moon has now moved into Scorpio. It is likely, too, that you will be receiving support from an unexpected source, and this delights you as you will discover that you have either a hidden admirer or a person who has been there for you even though you were totally unaware of the facts. It is always nice to know when we have someone on our team.

FRIDAY 3rd Today's Full Moon falls in the sign of Scorpio, and, because of this, you may need to go to the rescue of an old friend of yours. Somebody may be feeling out of sorts, or perhaps experiencing marital problems, and they can benefit from your sturdy shoulders and sound advice. Try to be there for them at some point today, even if you are not able to do so until later during the evening. The ground beneath this particular person has turned into quicksand and they need plenty of reassurance from a person such as yourself.

SATURDAY 4th Mercury has moved into retrograde action where it will stay until the 27th of this month. The period in between needs a great deal of caution when it comes to dealing with paperwork and also when travelling, as unnecessary complications could crop up if you are at all slapdash or careless. Also, watch what you say, you will have the unhappy knack of saying the wrong thing at the wrong time.

SUNDAY 5th Jupiter has now decided to join Mercury and move into retrograde movement which means from our position in space it appears to be going backwards. This could stir up a certain amount of insecurity for no reason whatsoever. Should this mood strike at any point, remember that it is only your imagination completely running away with you, and once you recognize the fact you will feel much more at ease.

MONDAY 6th The Moon has now moved into Sagittarius and, because of this, you will be well advised to listen to your gut feeling or your intuitions rather than that practical head of yours. Sometimes the inner voice has a way of putting us back on track when we seem to have strayed away into a miasma of confusion. This is certainly the case at this moment. A lot of good work, though, can be done quietly in the background.

TUESDAY 7th The Sun is in a beautiful aspect with Jupiter today. You may have a happy knack of being in the right place at the right time, and so will pick up on some kind of offer, or maybe a chance romance. There is a light-hearted feel about the day, and you decide it is time to put work out of your mind for a change and make some social arrangements for the immediate future. Your timing will prove to be perfect as others are only too keen to join you and help you have fun.

WEDNESDAY 8th Uranus, your money planet, has now decided to move into retrograde movement which could mean that, during the next few weeks or so, finances could get themselves into a bit of a muddle, unless you are able to draw on the common-sense side of your personality, and keep everything simple in this direction.

THURSDAY 9th The Moon in Aquarius could prove to be a bit of a drain on your resources, so, better let somebody else do the shopping whilst you turn your attention elsewhere. The Goat is normally a very sensible, practical creature, but can break out, and in so doing, is quite capable of inflicting a great deal of damage on his her or bank account.

FRIDAY 10th Someone may delight you today by behaving in an extraordinarily kind, considerate fashion, or perhaps they have decided to please you with a surprise present. Either way you are filled with a warm glow and your faith in humanity seems to have been restored. Good, because no man is an island and that includes you, no matter how self-sufficient you know you really are.

SATURDAY 11th Do think with greater care than usual when dealing with cash or business matters, and refuse to put your name to anything you are not completely happy with. Nothing is quite as it appears to be, even though you may have no obvious reason to suspect the motives of other people.

SUNDAY 12th Somebody may make a decision without your consent, despite the fact that it could affect your finances or ambitions. Luckily, this could lead to a much needed boost in some ways. However don't jeopardize your chances by making minor complaints because there is someone who would like nothing better than to see you make a glaring mistake. Be sure to take advantage of all opportunities while you can.

MONDAY 13th The planets' action today suggests that you really can't afford to make a mistake where money is concerned. Don't try to force your ideas down the throat of other people who clearly are on a completely different wavelength from yourself because if you do the situation could get out of control. This is an evening when you may find yourself defending your opinions rather than promoting them.

TUESDAY 14th Anything, or anyone, who tests your talents, and forces you to think along new and more adventurous lines should be encouraged today. Remember that you can't set your sights too high. Also bear in mind that partners may be suspicious of your motives, so don't make any major changes without first explaining what it is you are trying to achieve.

WEDNESDAY 15th The Sun is in a beautiful aspect with Mercury today, the planet of communication, minor changes and inspiration. Travelling is well-starred and new people you meet are likely to be important to you. If you have been neglecting paper-work, continue to do so, if it is not urgent until this planet resumes direct movement on the 27th.

THURSDAY 16th Don't be surprised if you find your-self plagued by groundless fears about the future. If you stop and regain your sense of perspective, you should be in no doubt just how much you have to look forward to in the next few weeks. Get out your realism Capricorn, you are certainly going to need it.

FRIDAY 17th Today's New Moon falls in the sign of Taurus, which is the fun area of life. An unexpected chance for romance, or perhaps an exciting social occasion, sets your heart fluttering. If you are a parent, this is an ideal time for taking decisions on behalf of children, because you will make a wise and proper choice.

SATURDAY 18th The Sun is in a beautiful aspect with Neptune and, because of this, you will find it hard to sit still for more than a few moments. You want to be in about six different places at the same time. If you are to make the most of this day, you will need to pause for thought and unjumble that mixed-up head of yours. Nevertheless, this can be an enjoyable as well as a romantic day.

SUNDAY 19th The Moon in Gemini could find you feeling a little under par. Perhaps you overdid it last night. Should this be the case, then this is an ideal Sunday for putting your feet up and really relaxing. Don't worry if others want to rush about. You just sit there, let the world drift away and carefully make some plans for the future.

MONDAY 20th Venus now moves into retrograde movement which could mean that matters related to your love life or creativity will become unnecessarily complicated, unless you go out of your way to keep matters as simple as possible. If you are a parent, a child may need some extra help and assistance. Try to ensure that you are there for them. Romantically, don't be fool enough to believe everything you are told.

TUESDAY 21st Today, the Sun moves into the sign of Gemini, and you begin about a month when your workload is likely to be extra heavy, particularly if you work in the service industries, health matters or charity work. The affairs of workmates will be more prominent and you may be supporting them through a rather difficult period. Your reward will come later on in the year.

WEDNESDAY 22nd Plans that have been made for some time now will finally get the go-ahead over the next couple of days. This in turn will create opportunities which other signs don't even know exist. Do take care not to antagonize other people, because you could easily make enemies out of friends, especially if they are already envious of your success, which is a distinct possibility.

THURSDAY 23rd Do take notice of what someone either much older or much younger has to say, because they are more in tune with what is going on than you are. As far as family and romantic relationships are concerned, try to control sarcasm, it will not aid your popularity. So, be extra careful what you say, because your words and your actions will have a wider implication than you realize.

FRIDAY 24th The answer to a domestic or cash dispute should reveal itself today. Even so, it may be a day or two before you are in a position to make the kind of changes you know are needed. In the meantime set new targets and look for ways to increase your earning power as well as your status.

SATURDAY 25th A wonderful aspect between Mars and Jupiter today suggests that you must be ready to take advantage of the lively prevailing circumstances which are around. There are plenty of opportunities to do yourself a bit of good emotionally, socially and maybe even workwise. The trick is being aware enough to recognize them when they present themselves.

SUNDAY 26th Although you would no doubt like to take everything you are told as gospel, you really must be careful where you place your trust. Cash and friends in particular should be kept as far apart as possible. The two simply won't mix. Put your own interests first for once, and don't feel you must rescue those who have got themselves into a fine old state, because they wouldn't have listened to your advice in the first place.

MONDAY 27th Luckily, Mercury resumes direct movement, so you can now feel free to push ahead with paperwork, documents and travel arrangements without fear of complications. Healthwise, if you have been under the weather you begin to regain strength and vigour. The Moon in Virgo suggests you may be hearing from somebody from abroad.

TUESDAY 28th   Something or someone is about to set you thinking in a new direction. You are becoming more understanding, aware and keen to get to know yourself. Don't think you have to follow other people; stay on familiar paths. Listen to what your instincts tell you, then start making the kind of progress that less intuitive people can only dream of.

WEDNESDAY 29th   Mercury is in a beautiful aspect with Mars today, providing you with the opportunity to take the initiative in all areas. Don't sit back waiting to see what will be done, take the lead and others will surely follow. On the home front, there seems to be plenty of news and movement, perhaps you are entertaining. If so you couldn't pick a better day.

THURSDAY 30th   The Moon in Scorpio suggests that you can gain today from meeting new people or making fresh contacts. This is no time to be stubbornly independent. You need other people as much as everybody else. It is simply that you are not prepared to admit it. However, this is a time for at least acknowledging this this to yourself.

FRIDAY 31st   An old friend seems to be instilling in you a new objective, and it is slowly beginning to form in your mind. Don't let it remain a dream. If you believe it has true potential, then start making some plans for the future in order to make this particular wish come true.

JUNE

SATURDAY 1st   The month begins a Full Moon and it occurs in the section of your chart which could stir up a certain amount of lowered self-esteem and confidence.

Be assured that all your worst imaginings are simply a figment of your imagination and the best way to offset all of this is to keep yourself as busy as possible. Dance the night away or take part in strenuous sports and you will retain your sense of perspective.

SUNDAY 2nd This seems to be an encouraging day for partnerships and relationships, and especially for artistic or creative pastimes. It seems, too, that a conflict of interest is about to solve itself in the best possible way. Other people will value your advice and admire your determination. Any chance to travel further afield should be snapped up.

MONDAY 3rd This is an ideal time for coming out into the open and being direct and forceful with those you would most like to impress. But be warned, if other people pick up on even the slightest hesitation on your part, then they may hold back from making any commitment. Advice from a close friend or colleague could prove invaluable today, but only if you are willing to put your opinions and prejudices aside and see things as they are, rather than how you would like them to be.

TUESDAY 4th It is unlikely that you will be able to reach the end of this particular day without some sort of unexpected development in your love life. You may be reluctant to place all your cards on the table, but it will be difficult to conceal your intentions any longer. You may have to resign yourself to a period of domestic conflict or an emotional tug of war with your lover.

WEDNESDAY 5th It is important today that you refuse to be fooled by superficial appearances. There is still a lot more water to flow under the bridge. Slowly, life will become less complex and the hostilities will be resolved in a friendly fashion, but it is simply a matter of time; fortunately you are the patient sort.

THURSDAY 6th Right at this moment it may seem to you life is all work and precious little play. But with Jupiter in retrograde movement in your sign, this is only to be expected. Still, you can take advantage of this time to put professional matters at the forefront of your agenda. This evening, don't fall into the bear-trap of believing the more money you spend the more fun you are going to have, this is a complete fallacy.

FRIDAY 7th Today has the potential for being one of the most inspiring days of the month and, if you keep your feet on the ground, as you usually do, you will be all the more successful. The Moon in Pisces gives off some powerful vibrations which suggest that the time may be right for a major transaction or purchase of some description.

SATURDAY 8th Mars is in a beautiful aspect with Neptune today. Peace and harmony can be found at home and, because of this, you may be reluctant to stray too far. Certainly it will be an ideal time for entertaining, and if you are fancy-free, this is a wonderful day for romance too; what starts out as a physical attraction soon turns into something much more important.

SUNDAY 9th You may feel today that a lot of little things are getting you down, and it is difficult to get a grip on the situation and think positively about the best way forwards. You seem to have come to the end of a cycle in life when people and things, no longer viable, can be discarded. Unfortunately, Capricorn sometimes finds it difficult to discard the past because of a hidden sentimental streak. Nevertheless, you are going to have to start considering this possibility.

MONDAY 10th   Venus is in a beautiful aspect with the Sun today and everybody around you should be in high spirits. It is an exceptionally good day for the creative person or those who are searching for love. Naturally, that special someone isn't going to bulldoze your door, so it is up to you to keep in circulation. Fight off a reclusive mood as it could prevent you from enjoying a wonderful evening.

TUESDAY 11th   Mercury is in aspect with inspired Neptune. Imagination, a sense of colour or design in your work or even the skill to solve problems are at your finger tips. There may be a tendency to become nostalgic or sentimental, perhaps something someone says or does takes you back in time. Nevertheless, you are practical enough to shake yourself back into the present and get on with what needs to be done.

WEDNESDAY 12th   Luckily, with Venus' current position, you should be able to prepare your ground effectively for a new lease of life. Relationships certainly appear to be important. Long-term plans, mind you, may have to be revised, in order to accommodate other people's needs. There will be decisions to make and it is vital that you take your time and make the right ones.

THURSDAY 13th   Mercury moves into Gemini where it will reside for a couple of weeks. This could have an effect on you physically, as your nerves may be jangling on occasions and, when this happens, it is important that you take some time out to rest up. On the working front, colleagues have some good ideas, and it will be worthwhile you taking them on board.

FRIDAY 14th Mars moves into the sign of Gemini today, where it meets up with Mercury. This is a warning for you not to overstretch yourself during the next couple of weeks or so. Certainly, your workload will be extra heavy, but if you pace yourself you will emerge hale and hearty. One word of warning: be especially careful with anything hot or sharp, particularly in the kitchen or the bathroom.

SATURDAY 15th Mercury is in a beautiful aspect with Mars today, and this galvanizes slacking grey cells into action. You have imaginative and creative ideas on what to do with your time, and others will be prepared to allow you to take the lead. If you are fancy-free, a strong physical attraction is likely right now, but don't mistake it for the 'real thing'.

SUNDAY 16th The New Moon today falls in the sign of Gemini and, because of this, it is likely that you may be socializing with workmates or receiving some interesting news, over the next couple of days, where professional matters are concerned. If it is necessary to begin a fresh cycle in life, then take it on because it will work out well for you. Romance is well-starred for the single.

MONDAY 17th It looks as if a number of interruptions or complications are stopping the flow of work or business. Still, although progress may be a bit slower, you can at least be sure that what you achieve now will endure, whether is concerns work or emotional matters. Just keep your wits about you, and don't expect too much too soon. Be prepared to commit yourself wholeheartedly.

TUESDAY 18th Mars is in a wonderful aspect with Uranus today and there may be some unexpected advantages which suddenly crop up completely out of the blue. The question is are you going to shilly-shally until they pass you by? I sincerely hope not. Finances are also likely to receive a shot in the arm, perhaps a long-awaited cheque in the post finally arrives.

WEDNESDAY 19th You seem to be withdrawing a little and, because of this, could miss out. For example, romantic partners may find it hard to reach you, but romance is still possible and partnerships are likely to receive a boost. This is a time to draw on inner resources to sustain you through this emotional period. Because of your current frame of mind, it might be a good idea to shelve practical decisions until another time.

THURSDAY 20th Uranus will soon be changing direction, and its capacity to shake your life up and cause volatile and unexpected events will slowly be increasing. Not that the influence is entirely one-sided. Intuition and perception will be at a premium too, and you will be at your sharpest and your most critical.

FRIDAY 21st Today the Sun moves into your opposite sign of Cancer, throwing the emphasis on your intense personal relationships but also suggesting that the next month is the time for co-operating more with other people, rather than insisting on striking out on your own, or that your way is the only way. Professional partnerships formed during this period are likely to be lucrative.

SATURDAY 22nd The astrological factors seem to suggest a lot of love, romance and opportunities, but you will need to be more tactful and patient if you want to secure the attentions of a new lover. This you seem hell-bent on doing. Avoid charging ahead like the proverbial bull in a china shop, rather, play the Goat that you are, and be prepared to take one step at a time towards this person of your dreams.

SUNDAY 23rd Mercury is in a beautiful aspect with Venus, and you are at your most idealistic at the moment. What is more, you are very sociable and ready to toss aside your inhibitions and worries and throw yourself either into romance or into the social whirl. And, when a Goat decides to have fun, the rest of the world had better watch out.

MONDAY 24th The Sun is at odds with your money planet, Uranus, today, therefore if you are supposed to be handling professional finances it might be better to enlist the help of somebody who can ensure that you don't make a wrong decision. If you are at home, and thinking of getting out and about, watch your possessions and don't pay inflated prices for goods, because bargains exist, all you need to do is hunt around.

TUESDAY 25th This seems to be a time for change and, although it may seem painful, it will lead to a period of new growth, so be ready to take advantage of anything that crops up, particularly if it happens quite suddenly. This evening it wouldn't be a bad idea to mix business with pleasure because loved ones will get on well with your workmates; just make sure they don't get on that little bit too well.

WEDNESDAY 26th Of course you are under Jupiter's bountiful influence at present. Because of this, colleagues and workmates will be a great support to you and, although you dislike relying on others, sometimes those around you can see more objectively than you can. Take a break where emotions are concerned and concentrate on finance and work. Movement on your chart indicates that a bit of short-term speculation could be lucky.

THURSDAY 27th This is as good a time as any to launch into the unknown, but also a time to strengthen what you already have and to reach new levels of understanding with those closest. Long-term plans will, in any case, be slow to reach fruition, and it is likely that endings rather than beginnings will characterize the next couple of days.

FRIDAY 28th Take life at a slower pace today and take care of your body, so that you ensure you remain healthy, fit and ready to deal with whatever challenges the planets may present you. You are generally a fit and healthy individual, but let's face it you do tend to bottle things up and often this reacts on your stomach. Perhaps it might be a good idea to let people know what you really think and then you will begin to feel better and more able to cope with any problems that are bothering you.

SATURDAY 29th Venus and Mars are in a beautiful aspect today, and so you are surrounded by peace and harmony both at home and at work. What more could you ask for? Social life looks promising too and there is likely to be a strong physical attraction which will set your heart pitter-pattering. But, if you already have a mate, it may set their pulses racing until they explode. So, much depends on your current situation as to whether or not this is a fantastic day.

SUNDAY 30th The Moon is in the fiery sign of Sagittarius, which is certainly stirring up your intuitions, your imagination and your ability to sense what somebody else's next move is likely to be. This is certainly a useful combination if you are trying to work out what a member of the opposite sex is really expecting from you. Of course, it will be easier for you to ask, but that simply isn't the Capricorn way, it's far too straightforward and places you in a vulnerable position, which you are not prepared to entertain.

JULY

MONDAY 1st The month starts off with a Full Moon in your sign, not altogether a great omen, but it is only for one day, so please don't get overly worried. Remember, too, that Full Moons are useful for putting the finishing touches to work or disposing of that which is no longer productive in your life, and that includes people.

TUESDAY 2nd At last, Venus decides to resume direct movement, therefore from now on creative and emotional affairs and those related to children, should all begin to run along smoother lines. Ambitions too will be easier to achieve on the working front. It is quite clear, Capricorn, it is a time to 'go for it'.

WEDNESDAY 3rd The Moon, in the financial area of your chart, puts the spotlight on shared resources and joint finances which come under scrutiny. But with happy influences you should be able to minimize confusion and maximize gains. Despite your obvious luck, take care to say what you mean and to listen attentively to other people. Failure to do so could mean that you will miss out in quite a big way, and that will be a pity.

THURSDAY 4th Clients, competitors and rivals at work will not hesitate to undermine your position should they be provided with a chance; it really is essential that you examine the smallest detail and explore every potential. Hold back on extravagance and choose secure solutions. Where love is concerned the stars will offer you the opportunity to successfully analyse problems.

FRIDAY 5th Your ruling planet, Saturn, is at odds with Mercury which certainly could lead to mental confusion and, because of this, you are advised to sidestep important decisions for the time being. Watch yourself in traffic, too, as you will have a tendency to wander mentally and this could lead to minor accidents. A little close attention will go a long way during this particular day.

SATURDAY 6th Today, Venus moves into the sign of Gemini. On the credit side, this will encourage you to find any excuse to celebrate as much as possible. On the deficit, this hints at a certain amount of stress which is likely to take its toll on you physically. Possibly you may decide that you are quite willing to pay for a hangover or a stomach upset providing you have the time of your life.

SUNDAY 7th The Moon in the fiery sign of Aries seems to suggest that you will be more than happy to potter around at home, entertain visitors or pay attention to the garden. Possibly last night took its toll on you, and you really need this particular day for replenishing yourself before you begin the working week. If you need a talk with a relative this is an ideal time for doing just that.

MONDAY 8th It is likely that you may be forced to face certain major issues over the next couple of days. You need to strike a balance between certain lifestyle ambitions, work issues, and your love life. Attention is also likely to focus on a partner or a mate. Passions will be intensified and it is best to confront and resolve any problems as quickly as possible.

TUESDAY 9th It looks as if you are in a situation which is vaguely familiar to you. Yes, you have been down this road before and, although you must pay attention to your emotional well-being, don't allow a partner to be the be-all and end-all of your life, because there is a possibility no matter how remote, that he or she may not be worth it. Something to be borne in mind.

WEDNESDAY 10th It is likely that you may have to sacrifice some free time in order to complete a business deal, or nourish a flagging relationship. A new admirer will boost your confidence, but your best bet is to pour your resources into an existing relationship, rather than something which is unlikely to be of any great importance. The best advice to you during this period is to remain as light-hearted as is possible.

THURSDAY 11th The Sun is in a beautiful aspect with Mercury today. This will give you confidence in your ideas and your ability to succeed. You certainly couldn't have a better time if you are doing any kind of travelling, dealing with legal matters or any kind of paperwork. This evening is a time for trying the new and different, rather than sticking to the same old faces and the same old places. Get yourself out of your rut, Capricorn, and be more experimental.

FRIDAY 12th Today there seems to be a more stable aspect in your love life which is replacing the earlier confusion you have experienced. There is a possibility too that a big occasion will give you the chance to push ahead a new business relationship or contact, and make some positive decisions. Do try to make sure though, that you don't stay up too late, because energy will begin to flag around ten o'clock.

SATURDAY 13th You are so busy with your ambitions at the moment that where your love life is concerned you could well have to justify why you are spending so little time with that special person, and why your priorities appear to be so muddled. If anyone tries to tie you down, somehow you will evade their grasp. However, all you are doing is putting off a confrontation which will only have to be faced at a later date, so why not take the bull by the proverbial horns and sort it out now.

SUNDAY 14th Mercury is in a challenging aspect with Neptune today. Therefore don't expect anything to go according to plan. Your direction seems to be muddled and confused, and in fairness it has to be said it seems to be caused by other people, rather than your good self. So, if you have travel plans do a little double checking before you leave home because you don't want to waste your time.

MONDAY 15th The New Moon today falls in the

intense personal area of your birth chart. For the fancy-free this could bring a new love interest, but if you are already in a relationship, it is likely that you may be preparing to take it a step further. Those of you who have been together for some time will be taking the opportunity to sort out recent differences, and will be slowly growing together as you should be.

TUESDAY 16th   Today Mercury is in a beautiful aspect with Pluto. This will make it a great deal easier for you to take on new ideas, or switch horses in mid-stream. One thing that is for sure is that routine will be almost impossible to stick to. You need to be very resilient.

WEDNESDAY 17th   Mercury is in a challenging aspect with Uranus. Because of this it is important that you refuse to sign financial documents as they are likely to lead to loss. Many of you will waste a good deal of time looking for possessions which seem to have gone 'walk about'. Try to ensure that you are your usual efficient self and you will save a lot of time as well as trouble.

THURSDAY 18th   Your ruling planet, Saturn, has now decided to change into retrograde movement. So, you could be in for a certain amount of frustration for a while, because for every step you take forward, you will feel it is necessary to take three backwards. Never mind, the stars are simply forcing you to learn from past experience before you reach out into life with anything or anyone new.

FRIDAY 19th   Today will provide you with the chance to first of all restore your equilibrium, and secondly give you a better chance to understand your partner's moans, concerns and groans. This will also give you plenty to think about on the cash front, and it is important you don't miss out on a major opportunity due to a lack of energy or planning.

SATURDAY 20th The Moon, in the earthy sign of Virgo, suggests that on a personal level you need to get to grips with fundamentals and approach people and situations in a direct and straightforward fashion. It is the only way you are going to get the answers to important questions. Socially, the further you travel today, the greater your chances of enjoying yourself. Don't be afraid to be adventurous.

SUNDAY 21st This may be a Sunday, but with the Moon in Libra, work keeps interfering with your social life. Should this flood over into your emotions, then that mate of yours may have reason to complain about your preoccupation as you seem to be a million miles away. Be sure you give loved ones your full attention.

MONDAY 22nd It might be a good idea to suppress certain thoughts and be as tactful as possible. Especially if you have any kind of investments. With Saturn in the property and family area of life, a professional front must be adopted if you are to reap the benefits of this influence. You are travelling down the road to success, which may call for some sacrifices, but this is something you, as a Goat, find relatively easy to take on.

TUESDAY 23rd The Sun is in a beautiful aspect with Pluto, and certainly if you are mixing with friends or acquaintances you are going to find them confident and in high spirits. This is just as well as you may be feeling a little down for one reason or another. However, time spent in their company will certainly be elevating you above petty difficulties, and giving you a more positive outlook on life.

WEDNESDAY 24th Today the Sun moves into the sign of Leo which is certainly good news for those of you who work in big institutions such as banks, insurance companies and the like; and good for the Goat who wishes to deal with such people. If you have been experiencing problems with officials or bureaucrats, the only thing you can do is be honest. In this way they are likely to smile more favourably upon you.

THURSDAY 25th Problems which have been with you since the early part of the year will begin to ease and you heave a sigh of relief. On a more personal level: handle lovers gently, especially if you are involved with a Piscean or a Virgoan. There will be some dramatic moments, but there is light at the end of the tunnel and it may be much nearer than you think. Just for once, you can be quite sure that there isn't a train coming in the opposite direction.

FRIDAY 26th Today, Mars moves into the sign of Cancer, which is of course your opposite number. If you are in a steady relationship, there could be a certain amount of tension developing. This could be due to that special person's frustration. However, if you use a good deal of charm, or plan a surprise, you will certainly escape a scene. If you are fancy-free, those hormones are coursing through your veins and physical attractions are likely to be the norm over the next few weeks or so.

SATURDAY 27th The Moon is in the fiery sign of Sagittarius which temporarily makes you run for cover. You need time to think about what your next move should be or perhaps to find an answer to an outstanding problem which has been plaguing you for quite some while. Instincts are certainly good though, and it might be a good idea to rely on them a little more than you usually do, particularly when in the company of strangers today.

SUNDAY 28th Today the Moon enters your sign, and so you are centre stage over the next couple of days. It is going to be very much a case of what Capricorn wants, Capricorn can get, and you shouldn't shirk from pushing yourself forward for a change. It is all very well being modest and preferring the background, but then when this occurs too often other people gallop off with all the glory.

MONDAY 29th The Moon continues in your sign, but at least it helps you to be more receptive to the suggestions and ideas of other people. What is more, in your personal life you will be responding from your emotions instead of your business-like head which, when it comes to the personal side of life, can often hold you back from getting closer to those you really care about.

TUESDAY 30th The Full Moon today occurs in the sign of Aquarius which is, of course, the section of your chart devoted to cash. Quite clearly then, you need to be a little careful; a source of income may be drying up, you may lose a possession, or, on a more positive side, a problem which has been bothering you for some time finally reaches an end. In any event it certainly isn't time for beginning anything new.

WEDNESDAY 31st The Moon continues in the sign of Aquarius, and it is a good time for sitting down with the special person in your life and making some plans for the future. However, this won't do any good at all unless both of you are being completely honest. Don't undermine other people's efforts by keeping back certain facts from them. If you do, this could lead to an unpleasant scene at a later date.

AUGUST

THURSDAY 1st The stars, today, suggest that you should try not to be taken in by the fanatical beliefs of other people. The only guidance you need at this moment is your conscience. Everything else can be totally disregarded. The Moon in Pisces is certainly going to keep you on the move from morning till night, but you seem to be stimulated by all of this activity. It is a good time for negotiations from which you will emerge triumphant.

FRIDAY 2nd Today Mercury moves into the earthy sign of Virgo, and you are provided with a couple of weeks which will be excellent for dealing with foreign affairs, or even long-distance travelling. Many of you will be at your most idealistic, and in your personal life, others don't have a hope of living up to your high expectations so you must be more realistic.

SATURDAY 3rd The stars are sure to set your imagination on fire. Provided you keep in touch with reality, you could discover something that gives you the edge over rivals and competitors. This evening you are likely to take refuge at home, as the Moon in Aries throws the emphasis on the family, suggesting you are unwilling to go too far for the sake of enjoyment.

SUNDAY 4th There are practical astrological reasons why you must stop being so accommodating, and instead, should put your own interests first. What takes place today, could mark the end of one particular phase or cycle in your life; a parting seems to be likely.

MONDAY 5th This is a time for assessing exactly where you are in your life and what your next move should be. One of the things to bear in mind though, is that you must simply let go of what has outworn its usefulness and is now redundant. Also, remember that it will be replaced when the time is right.

TUESDAY 6th Today is the day of the New Moon, and it occurs in the earthy sign of Taurus. Luckily for you, this is the area of life devoted to children, creativity, fun, pleasure and romance. A new beginning in one or more of these areas is likely to occur and you seem to have a great deal to look forward to. Remember that New Moons are always useful for beginning anything fresh, setting off in new directions and, generally, changing your mind if you see fit.

WEDNESDAY 7th Today Venus moves into the sign of Cancer. This, of course, is your opposite zodiac number and it throws its rosy glow over the intense personal side of life. If you are in a current relationship you may be preparing to take it a step further, and if you have decided to become engaged or married you have certainly picked a wonderful time. The fancy-free should get out and about over the next few weeks as they are certain to meet someone really special.

THURSDAY 8th Although you may be tempted to blame current difficulties on partners or workmates, remember that you make your own decisions and shape your own fate. On a different note, the stars suggest that your mind is working on altogether bigger things, in fact what others have rejected as impossible could turn out to be the inspiration you have been waiting for.

FRIDAY 9th It is likely that you have been swamped with responsibilities which, when all is said and done, should really not have been laid at your door. In short, you have permitted yourself to be used. Right now, the stars seem to suggest that your patience is at an end, and others had better look out for an explosion.

SATURDAY 10th Today, Pluto finally resumes direct movement and, where you may have had problems with friends and acquaintances who have perhaps been through a rough time, now they are beginning to make progress and are in a celebratory frame of mind. You can look forward then to a hectic few weeks of socializing and ebullient behaviour.

SUNDAY 11th It doesn't really matter whether your current problems are personal or professional, the thing you must remember is to start putting your own interests first, and, even more urgently, learning how to say no and to mean it. Too often those broad shoulders of yours have been used by others to weep on and lean on, but you cannot continue taking on the woes of other people. Besides, they must learn to stand on their own two feet sometime and now is as good as any.

MONDAY 12th The stars today suggest that you should try to avoid dwelling in the past. By all means it is important to learn from past mistakes, but don't dwell on them. There are occasions when your physical and emotional batteries might run low, and this is one of them. So, today's aspects are all about careful planning and conserving your energy for when you will need it the most. Too much effort could be self-defeating.

TUESDAY 13th It would be too easy for you to get trapped into a negative way of thinking, to believe that nothing is going right, and your situation can't possibly improve. Your outbreak of depression has probably been caused by insecurity, but nevertheless, it simply won't do. So, the trick you must learn is to view life as a whole, rather than getting bogged down in one small troublesome aspect of it.

WEDNESDAY 14th Venus is at odds with your ruling planet, Saturn, but this is fairly harmless. It simply means that there will be a tendency for you to go to excesses. So, if you are trying to stay trim and fit, then stick to your usual health regime and don't allow other people to lead you astray. If you are out socializing this evening, try to ensure that you get home at a decent hour because otherwise work will be suffering tomorrow.

THURSDAY 15th Your sign is frequently associated with money because you are so good at generating the stuff; what is more, you can certainly be relied on to be sensible when it comes to this side of life. But, this is not a good time to make promises you might later find difficult to honour. Even if it appears that you have been thinking along similar lines to a partner, the chances are that one of you has got the wrong idea entirely and this may have a potentially costly result.

FRIDAY 16th You may be tempted to blame current difficulties on partners or work colleagues. Remember that you make your own decisions and shape your own future, and nobody pushes a Goat around. Today, the Moon in Virgo certainly puts you in an adventurous mood and, wherever possible, you should be prepared to attempt the untried, the new, and the different.

This applies in your personal as well as in your professional life.

SATURDAY 17th It seems that you are going round in circles, asking the same questions over and over again. If you do this, then it shouldn't come as any surprise when you see the same old answers. This is a good time to try some lateral thinking and to decide to approach work and career and even partnership matters from a completely different angle.

SUNDAY 18th It is important today to make certain that you are receptive to other people, because it may well be that a loved one has stumbled upon something which you will be able to turn to your own advantage. With the Moon at the zenith of your chart, this is certainly a time for keeping a high profile and for putting forward ideas and suggestions to those who count. Don't be afraid to make a U-turn if you believe you have gone off on the wrong track.

MONDAY 19th Today you may need to dig deeper for solutions that are still missing even after hard thought in recent days. This is a time for long-term, substantial consideration. Take things at a slower pace, calm down and deal with your nervous energy.

TUESDAY 20th Try not to make too many demands on yourself today. Saturn in Aries has been causing you a certain amount of worry lately, all of it completely unnecessary. Do try to slow down and take stock, you are now so far ahead of everyone else, you could quite easily afford to take a day or two off if necessary.

WEDNESDAY 21st Mercury is in wonderful aspect with Neptune today. This sharpens up your intellect, increases your imagination and makes you more emotionally responsive to other people. No matter how crazy an idea may seem when you first think of it, jot down some notes, because, at a later date, you could realize there is a grain of genius in it which can be used to profit you in the very near future.

THURSDAY 22nd Today you may become suspicious of other people's motives, and perhaps with good reason. Jupiter in your sign, right now, can be deceptive, where cash matters and shared responsibilities are concerned. What takes place will force you to be more cynical about certain relationships. You may come to realize that your trust has been violated.

FRIDAY 23rd Today the Sun moves into Virgo. This means that you will go through a few weeks in a very idealistic frame of mind. Other Goats may get itchy feet, and become more adventurous. Those of you who are travelling during this period are sure to enjoy the experience and be making a good deal of fresh contact which will be useful for the future. It is a good time for you to consider taking on a fresh course of learning in the not too distant future.

SATURDAY 24th Over the past few days or so you seem to have devoted a great deal of time and effort to other people's needs, and not nearly enough to your own. Now the focus is back on what you want out of life, most importantly: partnership, social and travel arrangements. Above all, if you feel that a partnership or friendship has been drifting away from you recently, now is the time to do something about it, before the situation gets completely out of control.

SUNDAY 25th The Moon in your sign today certainly

puts you in a gentle and thoughtful frame of mind. This can work wonders for your romantic life, and it will also go down well with the family. Don't be surprised though, if you have a sudden urge to change long-made arrangements at the last moment. Luckily, other people are quite happy to go along with your change of heart.

MONDAY 26th   Mercury moves to the zenith of your chart into the sign of Libra. Over the next few weeks you can expect minor changes at your place of employment, and possibly important contracts will be signed too. Should you find there are new members of staff, then extend the hand of friendship.

TUESDAY 27th   The Moon in Aquarius does seem to suggest that money is coming and going a little too quickly. Try to balance the books so that you manage to retain some of the cash that is flowing in your direction. It might be a good idea to avoid the shops as an unusual bout of generosity and extravagance may descend and ravage your bank account like a robbery.

WEDNESDAY 28th   Today's Full Moon in the sign of Pisces advises you to take extra care when travelling from place to place. You may be late for appointments or there may be snarl-ups where traffic is concerned. Your mood, too, could be a little subdued, and no matter what your reactions may be to other people, you must vow not to take yourself or them too seriously for the time being.

THURSDAY 29th   Your money planet, Uranus, is in touch with Mercury. This could mean money in the mail, or perhaps a chance to swell the family coffers through a phone call. Any ideas that come to you completely out of the blue are certainly worth considering.

It might be a good idea to carry around with you a pen and pad, just in case you forget them at a later date. Money spent on romance or entertaining this evening will not be going to waste, you will certainly be getting good value for it.

FRIDAY 30th The Sun is in a beautiful aspect with Jupiter and this puts you in high spirits. In fact, everywhere you go, you seem to be greeted by sunny faces and willing hands only too keen to help you out. The whole day has a feeling of optimism and enthusiasm which carries on well into the evening when you are likely to get out and about with that special someone in your life.

SATURDAY 31st The Moon in Aries may confine you to base for one reason or another. Perhaps there is an emergency in connection with a relative, or maybe you are busy improving your surroundings. Other Goats may decide to throw an impromptu get together with friends, which proves to be successful. Not the best day in your life for romance, so if you are single get on the phone to friends.

SEPTEMBER

SUNDAY 1st The Moon in Aries seems to be suggesting that those closest to you definitely need some kind of reassurance from you before they will give their wholehearted support or even commitment. It is important you let them know you have included them fully in all your plans. Once you have done this you can go off and enjoy yourself as much as you please.

MONDAY 2nd Venus is in a tricky aspect with

Neptune today and you shouldn't believe everything you are told. Others may not be deliberately out to deceive you, but they could lead you up the garden path kicking and screaming. Keep those hooves of yours firmly on the ground and check everything you are told before you reach any important decision.

TUESDAY 3rd Venus and Mars are very cosy today making for a harmonious and happy twenty-four hours. There is peace and harmony in the family for a change and a chance for you to get out partying and perhaps even find romance. Should you meet someone new today, he or she is likely to be in your life for some considerable while. Plenty to look forward to then.

WEDNESDAY 4th Jupiter finally resumes direct movement today. Therefore, your intuitions are now steering you in the right direction and the only question is are you going to allow them to do so. Too often you prefer to rely on your grey cells which aren't always as dependable as you might think. For the remainder of the year, listen to that still, inner voice before you make a major move.

THURSDAY 5th Unfortunately, Mercury has decided to go into retrograde movement which it will maintain until the 27th of the month. Therefore, during the interim period, you need to take care and do a great deal of double checking if you are involving yourself in travelling, legal matters or paperwork. It is the only way to avoid trouble. It's worth putting yourself out; if you don't you will certainly live to regret it.

FRIDAY 6th The Moon in Gemini is going to have something of a draining effect on you. It might be a good idea to rest up a little more than is usually the case, particularly if you are planning to go out this evening. Otherwise you may be unable to keep your eyes open once the clock strikes nine. This will be a pity, as you could miss out on a good deal of fun.

SATURDAY 7th Venus and Pluto are in excellent spirits today, and so are your friends, acquaintances and contacts. Don't be too independent; ask for advice if and when you need it. Struggling on alone may be very grown-up, but it can be a lonely path to travel, and others, right now, can point you in the direction of a few short-cuts.

SUNDAY 8th If your energy is down a little, don't let companions land all responsibility on your shoulders. Do what you can, but give yourself time to think about boosting your stamina and, above all, go in for a little bit of pampering. Stick close to familiar surroundings this evening; you won't be at your most adventurous.

MONDAY 9th You are certainly not going to let any-one or anything stand in your way today, that is for sure. Your light-hearted mood will draw the brighter people of life to your side, so the conversation should whiz along. Just make certain you are keeping the peace where it really matters, which is basically amongst the family and other loved ones.

TUESDAY 10th Mars is lining up in a dynamic way with Pluto. Try not to be too self-sufficient today, because friends and contacts have the knack of being in the right place at the right time, and they possess the information you need before you can proceed further.

WEDNESDAY 11th Mercury lines up with Uranus

and many of you may be signing on the dotted line where an important contract is concerned. Mind you, for some an extravagant mood may descend and, although this is very rare, when it does occur it does considerable damage. Best then to stay away from temptation and let other people do the shopping while you occupy yourself elsewhere.

THURSDAY 12th The New Moon falls in the sign of Virgo today. Splendid if you are starting a new course, great if you are going on any kind of long trip, and good too for pushing ahead with legal matters. You are at your most adventurous and ready to surprise a few people who thought they knew you well. Too often, Capricorn, you are thought of as being a little 'stodgy', which is far from the truth, because you can be as silly or as adventurous as anybody else and others are about to find out today.

FRIDAY 13th Mars is now in the sign of Leo which strongly suggests that you bear a healthy respect for bureaucrats and officials who will make your life a misery if you fail to do so. Don't flaunt rules and regulations, abide by them as you usually do, and you won't experience any difficulty whatsoever. Mind you, this placing of Mars could certainly be stirring up the hormones of the opposite sex, so you had just better watch out.

SATURDAY 14th During the next few days the emphasis is likely to be on the affairs of a brother or sister, short trips and everything connected with the media. Your brain will be working overtime and, if your job depends on creativity, you will certainly be putting in a good account of yourself. Romance will be flirty this evening, but don't overdo the attention-seeking; if you have a mate, there may be complaints.

SUNDAY 15th It is possible that you may have to stand still or at least pause to reflect for a couple of days until you find the answers to important questions. There is no sense in skimming the surface of matters or things, or looking for short cuts through experiences. Make sure you are not clinging too firmly to old memories. This is an inclination of the Goat, which tends to be rather attached to the past in one way or another.

MONDAY 16th The Moon, at the zenith of your chart, suggests you should keep a very high profile particularly where work is concerned. Don't be shy about pushing yourself forward, otherwise someone else may gallop in and steal your thunder, and that would never do. If you want to make changes on the professional level, this is an ideal time for doing just that.

TUESDAY 17th It looks as if you are looking ahead in a friendly and open fashion, knowing that certain people in your life will be there for you when or where you want them. Your confidence is bouncing higher and higher, despite a secret nagging feeling that one argument or debate has still yet to be settled. The time of reckoning will come fairly soon.

WEDNESDAY 18th The Sun is in a beautiful aspect with Neptune today and this will be stirring up your grey matter and perhaps keeping you on the go physically too. The Goat who finds it necessary to stay in one place for any length of time could become easily bored, and therefore irritable. But if you can find plenty to stimulate you, this can be a great day which will lead on to a sentimental and rather nostalgic evening, which you will thoroughly enjoy.

THURSDAY 19th   You are likely to have some bright ideas that pop into your head quite unexpectedly. These you will need to get across to either workmates, family or other loved ones. Sometimes you run ahead of yourself, but you need to slow right down, pause, reflect and come to a sensible conclusion. This shouldn't be difficult for you as common sense is second nature.

FRIDAY 20th   Your money planet, Uranus, is in good aspect with Pluto today, and so any changes you make to a financial plan are likely to be good, providing you use your intuition as well as your practical common sense. It might be a good idea to involve yourself in a little investigation, digging around in the background of things before you make any important move. You will be surprised what you will be able to turn up.

SATURDAY 21st   The Moon in your sign is eventually driving home to you that relaxing is possible even in these highly stressed times. So, pick the right companions who will support you in whatever you choose to do. There is a certain gentleness and softness about you today which others will find attractive and they will do their very best to please you in all areas of life. This could be a heart-warming day.

SUNDAY 22nd   I think it is time to allow yourself to coast along, for this particular day, thinking quietly about highly personal matters. If you are dragged into other people's business you will only end up bored, or worst still resentful, and then you might say something that could upset them. So protect yourself until you are feeling a little stronger and ready to push ahead. If you have a special someone in your life, you can be quite sure that all of your emotional needs will be met in full at the moment.

MONDAY 23rd The Sun moves into the sign of Libra and so begins the most ambitious time of the year for you. The only problem is that as a Goat you tend to go way over-the-top and then other people close to you begin to feel they are being neglected. Try to strike an even balance and you will be able to avoid this pitfall.

TUESDAY 24th Looking to the long-term is not easy for you at the moment, as almost everything seems to be a little dreary and depressing, but this is not true, it is merely the reflection of your own mental attitude at this moment. Try then to find a different way of communicating with workmates or team companions. Co-operation is all during this particular day. This evening, don't spend in order to impress other people, it will prove to be a complete and utter waste of time.

WEDNESDAY 25th Trying to sort out close relationships in your life is an uphill struggle at this time. You keep finding people wanting, yet you also know perfectly well that you can't travel solo, so try to be tolerant. Always remember, Capricorn, that nobody is perfect and this certainly includes you. Therefore, you have no right expect perfection in other people.

THURSDAY 26th If you can find time to be on your own, so much the better. This is a fast-moving time which lies ahead and you may be able to use the next few days or so in order to wind down. You must also respect confidences if you are asked to help sort out a tricky problem of a colleague, friend, or maybe even a loved one. To betray them will only rebound on you at a later date.

FRIDAY 27th Today is the day of the Full Moon and it occurs in the fiery sign of Aries. Do take care that you don't upset relatives, it will be all too easy to do. Other people do not always live up to your high expectations, nor do they have the stamina or endurance for which you are so renowned. Tolerance is something you will need during this particular day.

SATURDAY 28th Mercury has finally decided to see common sense and resume direct movement. Therefore you need not fear signing documents, travelling or even pushing ahead with legal matters. You may also discover that you have been thinking along the wrong lines where a long-standing problem is concerned and so develop a strong urge to kick yourself for being such a fool.

SUNDAY 29th The Moon is in the sign of Taurus which is, of course, the pleasure-seeking, fun area of life. It won't do any harm either if you happen to be creative because ideas will be bouncing off your walls. Romantically though, don't overdo the flirty bit or you may upset someone close to you.

MONDAY 30th The Moon in Taurus seems to suggest that emotionally you are a little stressed and somewhat confused. Don't allow loved ones to lean on you or to distract you, but insist on doing your own thing, in your own good time. There have been too many long-running disagreements recently and you need space to find a solution. Don't neglect your social life this evening, though, because you are also in the mood for letting rip.

OCTOBER

TUESDAY 1st Although on the outside you appear as confident as ever, on the inside your emotions are churning over. No wonder; if workmates, loved ones and employers seem determined to take everything you say and do the wrong way, your best course of action is to do as little as possible and wait for the difficulties to calm down.

WEDNESDAY 2nd The Sun is at odds with Jupiter at the moment and therefore your judgement could be poor. The best thing to do is to shelve important decisions for the time being, particularly if they involve official or bureaucratic matters. Instead, give yourself over to enjoyment, but even then don't go to excess.

THURSDAY 3rd If you haven't accepted some kind of deal, pay off or contract which has been offered recently, then don't be surprised if the offer is withdrawn soon. Naturally, you may be relieved that the decision is taken out of your control. It is never easy for a Capricorn to give up something they come to rely upon or even trust. On this occasion at least, you could do with a little push in the right direction.

FRIDAY 4th Venus, today, moves into the sign of Virgo which is very nice if you can afford to go travelling, because you would most certainly find romance. However, at home, there may be a chance of romance with someone from foreign climes. Conversely, if you are already in a relationship it is likely that you are being so idealistic that the person with whom you are involved hasn't a hope of living up to those high expectations.

SATURDAY 5th   A dramatic change in your circumstances is indicated soon, and all you have to do now is to sit back and let the stars take their course. Despite this, a little more caution is needed in partnership affairs. The stars indicate that some kind of long-term commitment may be hard to avoid, but much as you hate the idea of being tied down, you might be willing to relent at this time.

SUNDAY 6th   Finally, Neptune decides to see common sense and resume direct movement. So, short trips and journeys will be much more straightforward, meetings and negotiations more successful and, relationships with a brother or sister or both, will be improving in leaps and bounds.

MONDAY 7th   Today's aspects are likely to exert a rather odd influence on many Goats, and the stars will have the most loving Goat ready to make some changes. Remember though, there is always someone who is stronger, bigger and better connected than you, so don't start a fight unless you stand a fair chance of winning it. Even better, get someone influential to back your cause.

TUESDAY 8th   This is not a time for taking unnecessary risks. In fact, your best plan by far right now, is to watch the rules and make sure you do nothing which will get you noticed. You may feel a little lonely or isolated, but there are still some people you can trust, an older or more experienced colleague perhaps, if he or she is approached in the right way. They would be very happy to pass on some valuable wisdom and advice.

WEDNESDAY 9th   Mercury today moves into the sign

of Libra which is, of course, the zenith of your chart.
Minor changes are likely to be taking place at work, and
there may even be rumours of an important contract.
New members of staff who may appear should be
greeted with a warm welcome.

THURSDAY 10th At last your money planet, Uranus,
resumes direct movement. So, for the rest of the year,
financial matters will run along much smoother lines.
No surprises or set-backs to rock you on your heels.

FRIDAY 11th If you discover that bosses or workmates
are openly hostile to your plans or your ambitions, it
is, nevertheless, time to press on. The more stubbornly
you cling to your hopes and ambitions, the much
greater chance you will have of achieving them. You
enjoy a challenge, of course, and nothing would give
you greater pleasure than to prove all of your critics
hopelessly wrong.

SATURDAY 12th Today is the day of the New Moon
and it occurs at the zenith of your chart. Prepare
for some exciting changes where work matters are
concerned. This is an ideal time, being a Saturday,
for making plans for the future because, very soon,
you will be able to put them into operation. Socializing
with people from work will also work out well and could
also lead to romance.

SUNDAY 13th The Moon in Scorpio suggests that you
spend this Sunday in the company of friends involved
with team sports or perhaps visiting a club. If you are
single these are the most likely places where you could
meet someone rather special. Make this a light-hearted
day though, avoid looking for heavy commitment from
anyone, otherwise you could be disappointed.

MONDAY 14th It seems that attention to detail is the way to success during this particular day. In fact, if you let your mind stray for even a moment you could miss out on something vitally important. The stars suggest that you can learn as much from partners' or colleagues' mistakes as you could from your own, with none of the pain or embarrassment that they experienced.

TUESDAY 15th Domestic and partnership problems seem to be under a large, dark cloud and nothing you say or do seems likely to restore peace for the time being. But don't get rattled; keep telling yourself that loved ones will come round sooner or later, and they will. Some sort of showdown is indicated soon, but on this occasion at least, you really should be grateful for the chance that it gives you to clear the air.

WEDNESDAY 16th The Moon in the fiery sign of Sagittarius will be strengthening your intuition, imagination and ability to concentrate on research that may be needed in order to get a project off the ground. In your personal life, listen to your hunches and **try** to suss out people's moods.

THURSDAY 17th If your best plans go wrong today, take it as a sign that you must lower your sights and build up slowly towards achieving what you want. Remember, too, that if old methods no longer appear to work, it is time you replace them with something more modern, even if it means abandoning half-finished plans and projects and starting from scratch.

FRIDAY 18th The Moon in your sign makes you more receptive to the ideas and suggestions of other people and their ideas which will make your mind boggle. It is an excellent time for making all sorts of changes and, where you normally use your grey cells when responding to other people's suggestions, now you are using your emotions and this subtle approach will certainly be making you much more receptive as well as popular.

SATURDAY 19th While one of your first impulses today may be to jump on a boat and leave your worries behind you, the eternally practical side of you will realize that it is not a serious alternative yet. So, accept your present circumstances for what they are and face domestic and career problems with courage and confidence.

SUNDAY 20th The stars today suggest that the longer you wait for something, the more satisfying your eventual rewards will be. The Moon in Aquarius puts you in something of an extravagant mood. So, if you are wise, you will allow other people to do the shopping, while you stay firmly at home. Money spent on entertainment may not necessarily give you good value.

MONDAY 21st If it is your job to balance the books on the working front, then take care because you could be easily distracted and make mistakes. For those at home: continue to stick to your budget otherwise you will have reason for regret at a later date. Those in the professions will be only too happy to give you some advice which is badly needed, so why don't you give them a call?

TUESDAY 22nd The danger now is that you could easily allow a romantic affair to lead you astray, when there are so many other things demanding your attention. Luckily, the stars will help you to keep something in reserve, even though it may only just be enough.

Partners and loved ones will gladly take everything you have to offer today, but don't count on getting much in return.

WEDNESDAY 23rd Today, the Sun enters the sign of Scorpio which is the area of life that represents acquaintances, contacts and objectives. So, it is quite clear that you are going to need other people more than is usually the case. Information passed on by them will be invaluable, so try to avoid being too independent. We all need other people some time, and it looks as if it is now your turn.

THURSDAY 24th The Sun today is at odds with your money planet, Uranus, and, where cash matters are concerned, you could go completely over-the-top. Try to be your usual thrifty self. Avoid so-called bargains and stay well away from the shops if at all possible. When it comes to work, leave the drawing up of budgets to someone else as you are simply not in the right frame of mind and could make mistakes.

FRIDAY 25th Mercury is in a beautiful aspect with Mars, and this seems to suggest a certain amount of movement and good news among the family. You, yourself, won't be content to sit still for very long either. You want fresh challenges, fresh faces and fresh scenes to stimulate you. Romance is flirty but fun, and because of this shouldn't be taken too seriously.

SATURDAY 26th The Full Moon today occurs in the sign of Taurus which seems to hint that a cancellation of a social occasion or even a date may occur. If so, bite your lip and swallow the disappointment. This may be unavoidable and has nothing to do with yourself; rather outside influences and circumstances have caused this to happen. Nevertheless, as always, Full Moons are good times for putting the finishing touches to anything.

SUNDAY 27th Mercury's move into Scorpio suggests that you will be making new friends and contacts during the next few weeks or so, and very useful they are going to be too. It is possible that they may be a good deal younger than yourself but this is no excuse for ignoring their pearls of wisdom. If you do, you will certainly regret it at a later date.

MONDAY 28th Your ruling planet, Saturn, is in lovely aspect with Pluto so the mood upon you is one of change. However, ensure that you don't make changes simply for the sake of it. Conversely, if you have been waiting for an ideal time to move off or move in, or for making an important decision, then it has arrived, so make sure you don't waste it. Friends will be great company this evening.

TUESDAY 29th The Moon is in Gemini and this could leave you a little exhausted. It is likely that work is a bit frantic, and colleagues perhaps very demanding. It might be a good idea for you to put your foot down if you suspect for one moment that you are being taken for granted. Stand firm, but use charm.

WEDNESDAY 30th Venus enters the zenith of your chart and throws a rosy glow over professional matters. If you happen to be single you may even become involved romantically with a work colleague over the next few weeks or so. If you are artistic you will be doing very well for yourself.

THURSDAY 31st Venus lines up with Pluto today,

and you will find that friends, acquaintances and contacts have some useful information to pass on to you. Don't be too proud to listen to what they have got to say, because this could lead to great enrichment in the near future.

NOVEMBER

FRIDAY 1st Even those friends of yours who thought they knew you well will wonder what has happened to you right now, as ideas and opinions you have been keeping to yourself come rushing out. But you, above all, should know that it simply isn't possible to succeed in everything, so concentrate on those one or two things which are important to you, and don't be offended if other people make use of the things you discard.

SATURDAY 2nd Family and cash matters can safely be left to take care of themselves for a while. In fact, the aspects today make it clear that you have been fretting for no good reason. Creatively, you are now in a good position to turn your long-term dreams and ambitions into reality. All it takes is confidence which, deep in your heart, you intuitively know is there.

SUNDAY 3rd Mars and Pluto are in something of an explosive mood today, so you need to take care when in the company of acquaintances and friends, as it won't take much to offend them. Luckily, you are a cautious person. Nevertheless, you may be called on to pick up the pieces when a close friend has a dispute with somebody who isn't quite as tactful as youself.

MONDAY 4th Whatever you set your mind to over

the next few days has an excellent chance of success. Be ambitious in all you do and refuse to accept second best. The stars are currently working in your favour. Remember, too, that anything which increases your knowledge and understanding may also increase your earnings.

TUESDAY 5th The stars are good today for getting things done or organizing your time more efficiently. You could hardly wish for a better set of circumstances. So, plan ahead more, and make a point of clearing up the backlog of jobs you have started, but never quite finished.

WEDNESDAY 6th Instead of dwelling on the inevitable mistakes from the past, try to keep your attention on the good things which are still coming in your direction. It will be the easiest thing to lose heart, and so it is absolutely imperative that you manage to maintain a positive outlook on life.

THURSDAY 7th The stars suggest that you may be confronted by situations that need commitment, courage and a degree of aggression, not usually associated with your sign. Relationships of all kinds are about to go through a period of change, but you will profit from this process only if you accept that progress must happen if you are to discover what you want out of life.

FRIDAY 8th Though there is still a great deal to do before you can feel completely secure, the overall picture should now be a lot more confident. Also, you are feeling happier about your finances. The stars today give you plenty of energy and enthusiasm. All that you need is to push ahead with the changes you feel necessary.

SATURDAY 9th Romantically and creatively, and even cashwise, this promises to be an incredible day. In fact, you haven't been in such a strong position for a long while and it is a time which you should use for making changes and inspiring both yourself and others to new achievements. Even if partners don't seem to share your enthusiasm, it won't be long before your sense of fun wins them around.

SUNDAY 10th Your ruler the Sun, is beautifully aspected by Uranus which is your money planet. This could be a very profitable time. It may only come in the form of opportunities for the future, or perhaps some nice presents, but either way don't look a gift horse in the mouth. You have a special charisma about you today, and are very attractive to the opposite sex.

MONDAY 11th The New Moon in the sign of Scorpio certainly will be creating a good deal of activity in your friendship circle. Any chances to join them socially this evening should be snapped up. They may make some interesting introductions which you could certainly use to help you to achieve your ambitions.

TUESDAY 12th You won't be feeling quite as restricted as you have been lately, and you should be looking for ways to make the most of unique ideas and insights. But, although the stars indicate that anything is possible, don't waste time on projects which have little practical value. Remember that a short cut is often the quickest route to somewhere you didn't really want to go to in the first place.

WEDNESDAY 13th The Moon in Sagittarius is certainly stirring up your intuition, and all you have to do is persuade yourself to listen just for a change. Common sense, of course, has its place in this life, so does that 'gut' feeling, which often has the edge over the logical side of our brains. Make sure you use it today.

THURSDAY 14th The Moon in your sign makes you more receptive to the ideas and suggestions of other people. What is more, you are far more emotionally moved and this is very attractive to that special someone in your life, and also to other potential admirers.

FRIDAY 15th Mercury moves into Sagittarius today. This seems to suggest that during the next few weeks or so you are going to be busying yourself in the background of things: rooting around and trying to find out what is really going on in situations at work, within the family and where lovers are concerned. You may find some good news, you must also be prepared for something which could surprise you.

SATURDAY 16th Venus is in a beautiful aspect with Pluto today. It is difficult for you to imagine getting through the day without thinking about making a change of direction, particularly where career matters are concerned. Luckily, though, it is a weekend so if you can't implement these plans for the time being, you are afforded a chance to think twice.

SUNDAY 17th The Moon in Aquarius could put you in an extravagant mood. There is no need to spend a great deal, particularly if you are hoping to impress other people. All you need be is your usual self; even if it means playing the giddy Goat, others will certainly appreciate it.

MONDAY 18th Any travel plans you have should have a serious purpose to them if you are to enjoy to the full what you find at the end of your journey. You seem to be desperate to keep on the move, but the stars warn you that resources are limited. So, be ready to economize. Someone from a different background will have a deep effect on you, perhaps even force you to question beliefs that are taken for granted.

TUESDAY 19th The Moon in Pisces continues to stir up a certain amount of restlessness. You seem able to quell this by making short trips and visits both of a professional and personal nature. Whilst on the go, brief encounters of a romantic nature are quite likely. But don't imagine that this is the love of your life. Simply regard it as a harmless flirtation and then be prepared to wait and see.

WEDNESDAY 20th The Moon moves into the family and property areas of life and, if you want to make any changes here, this is the ideal time for doing just that. Those of you who want to entertain at home this evening couldn't have picked a better time. You are on sparkling form and will be gleaning garlands for your ability as a host or hostess.

THURSDAY 21st It would be no surprise to find you plotting revenge against those who have let you down or betrayed your trust. But, before taking any drastic action, make sure you know all the facts, otherwise you could easily find yourself in a costly, as well as embarrassing, position.

FRIDAY 22nd The Sun moves into the sign of Sagittarius today, and it is that time of the year when you would do better keeping a low profile involving yourself in research or investigating facts in connection with your job. The recluse within you is surfacing, and you will be putting your time to good use with hobbies and maybe one or two people you have been neglecting for quite some time now. Nevertheless, although it may be relatively quiet on the social front, in all other areas you are advised to rely on your instincts, rather than your grey cells.

SATURDAY 23rd Today, Venus moves into Scorpio and any recent disagreements between yourself and your friends can be easily healed at this time. Mind you, they will probably have to come and find you, because you are keeping a rather low profile at this time. Nevertheless, you will enjoy kissing and making up and sitting down and having a good gossip about mutual friends.

SUNDAY 24th The Sun is in a beautiful aspect with Pluto today and so the theme of friendship continues at this time. Your oldest friends have great confidence and are willing to help you in any way they can, all you have to do is ask, which is not too easy for a Goat, because, let's be honest, you have tremendous pride, though few are aware of this fact. Generally speaking, you like to be independent but everybody needs somebody some time, and this looks to be one of those occasions.

MONDAY 25th Today is the day of the Full Moon, and it may lay you low with a minor bug, or perhaps a bout of exhaustion. Whichever applies it is certainly time to take it easy; don't overcrowd your routine with too much. Take things at a steady pace, and then this evening you can relax in the company of your loved ones or lover. As usual a good time for putting the finishing touches to situations and ideas.

TUESDAY 26th It may feel to you that other people are ranging themselves against you. On the other hand, the stars urge you to make the most of all that is happening to you. You have much to look forward to between now and the end of the year, don't jeopardize it by overreacting.

WEDNESDAY 27th The Moon is in your opposite sign of Cancer, and so for the next couple of days you are advised to co-operate with other people wherever you possibly can. This is not a time for independent moves. You need to consult and discuss moves before pushing ahead. Failure to do so could lead to a certain amount of disagreement.

THURSDAY 28th If you are fancy-free you have a couple of days when there is a strong possibility of meeting someone new. If you are in a steady relationship and things have gone a little sour, now is the ideal time for planning a surprise and trying to ginger up some excitement between you. A walk down memory lane could be a good idea, or perhaps you could physically go and visit a place you haven't been to for some years.

FRIDAY 29th The Moon continues in Cancer and circumstances in your intense personal relationships tend to fluctuate a good deal. Nevertheless, this will keep you on your toes. If you are single, this is an ideal time for meeting fresh faces, but don't automatically assume that you have met Romeo or Juliet, it may simply be a case of finding a good friend and, let's face it, we all need some of those.

SATURDAY 30th The Moon in Leo warns you against breaking the law in any way. In your instance it is likely to be a case of drinking and driving, but now that you have been warned you have no excuse. Get somebody else to ferry you around if you are determined to get legless. If you are staying at home with that special someone, you will be reacting more emotionally to what they have to say than is usually the case and, as a result, could be nursing hurt feelings. Don't hug them to yourself, let the other person know exactly what you are experiencing. I think you will find they will warm to you.

DECEMBER

SUNDAY 1st Aspects today may coincide with the loss of something you once relied on. If so, you can be absolutely certain that it is no longer right for you, or even needed. Alternatively, maybe a partnership or relationship has disappointed you in some way, or failed to meet your expectations. If so, ask yourself if it really matters, and if you really care. If not, then the time has come to move on to meet someone new.

MONDAY 2nd If what you are currently experiencing is not entirely to your liking, then the aspects today will give you the opportunity to ask a few searching questions. If you don't receive the answers you were hoping for, by the end of the week, don't be afraid to walk away. The stars suggest a better deal can easily be negotiated somewhere else.

TUESDAY 3rd At last, your ruling planet, Saturn, has decided to go into direct movement. This means that slowly, over the next few days, you begin to lose that one step forward half a dozen steps back feeling that you have been suffering for quite some time now. It is a bit like walking up a down escalator.

WEDNESDAY 4th Mercury is in a challenging aspect

with your ruling planet Saturn, and this could make you a little too absent-minded or your concentration may be poor. Don't overload yourself with work today, simply stick to routine and make sure everything you tackle is completed satisfactorily. This evening you may very well feel it is time to put your feet up and if so, why not?

THURSDAY 5th That active planet, Mercury, has finally moved into your sign. This will enliven your self-expression, keep you more physically active, and fill your head with inventive and creative ideas. Physically, too, you will want to be on the go as much as possible, and the weeks ahead promise to be packed full of movement and excitement.

FRIDAY 6th The Moon enters the zenith of your chart, and you certainly seem to be the star on the working front. It looks as if you have been a rather clever Capricorn in some way and now may be gathering in the garlands; you certainly deserve them. Others of you may want to make minor changes to your ambitions.

SATURDAY 7th You may be in a sensitive mood today, and you could easily destroy the atmosphere with a careless word or gesture. Disagreements will be petty and short-lived, but they could also have unforeseen consequences. So, apply some of that famous Capricorn self-discipline and refuse to be drawn into arguments which no one can win and everybody may regret.

SUNDAY 8th The Moon in Scorpio urges you to avoid any wishful thinking right now, and look for a more realistic footing for your ambitions. This applies to most

areas of daily life, and in particular to career, finances
and your friendship circle. Accept who you are, and
where you are, and imagine where you would like to
be in approximately six months' time.

MONDAY 9th　Venus and Mars are in a beautiful
aspect today so it promises to be a hectic but exciting
day on the working front, and you will have plenty of
energy left this evening for enjoyment. Other people
will sense your good humour and will be throwing
invitations at you. Certainly, a promising time if you
happen to be fancy-free because you could start a mad
infatuation, and why not?

TUESDAY 10th　The New Moon today falls in the sign
of Sagittarius; your instincts are almost psychic and it
is important you back them to the hilt both today and
tomorrow. You really can't go wrong in this area but
the only problem is whether you can trust yourself. I
certainly hope so because that is the way you should
be travelling.

WEDNESDAY 11th　The Moon in your sign puts you
at the centre of all the activity over the next couple of
days. You are very much the puppeteer pulling the
strings from the wings, and dictating the tune that
others will dance to. Don't let this feeling of power
go to your head, otherwise you will find yourself very
unpopular.

THURSDAY 12th　You are a little more touchy today,
and sensitive. Where you need logic you use emotion,
where you need emotion you use logic; things seem to
be a little bit higgledy-piggledy and it is up to you to try
and think first before you act or react to other people or
situations.

FRIDAY 13th A good day for making minor changes in any area you choose. It is particularly good if you want to change your appearance or image, take on a fresh line of study or interest or maybe some creation which hitherto you haven't tried. Be experimental and enjoy yourself.

SATURDAY 14th The Sun is at odds with Mars today and you may find yourself in the thick of arguments without any clear knowledge of how they began in the first place. This is particularly true when you are dealing with relatives at home, so, be extra careful and diplomatic when you find yourself in their company, and escape this evening to the company and comfort of friends.

SUNDAY 15th The Moon in the financial area of your chart suggests that a bout of extravagance could descend. Possibly this is because you are out doing your Christmas shopping; ensure that you stick to the very strict list you made and don't allow anything or anyone to tempt you into extravagances you can ill afford.

MONDAY 16th Everyone, of course, has their time of worry, but you have let your doubts and suspicions get the better of you. Part of the problem stems from the fact that friends and workmates seem rather distant. A fact likely to be compounded on this particular day. Just keep telling yourself that set-backs and disputes are part of life.

TUESDAY 17th Venus today moves into the sign of Sagittarius. Oh dear! This could put the cat amongst the pigeons. There is a strong tendency for you to become involved with people who are being anything but honest with you, for example married men or

women. So take a few precautions before you accept
a second date, make it your business to establish once
and for all whether or not there is somebody waiting for
your date at home. If so, 'exit stage right' immediately
as this really isn't a situation you can cope with.

WEDNESDAY 18th Someone you usually get along
with very well now seems to be putting your patience
to the test, and for no apparent reason. The chances are
you are being deliberately provoked just to see how you
will react. No matter how difficult or obstructive others
may be, don't lose your temper. A new beginning is
just over the horizon, and you really can't afford to
jeopardize it.

THURSDAY 19th Aspects indicate that your energy
levels may be a little low, so don't overdo it. Stay with
methods and routines you are familiar with, and don't
allow yourself to be talked into trying anything outrageous. Career and cash matters ought to be handled
with tact, as workmates and employers are inclined to
change direction or change their minds for no apparent reason.

FRIDAY 20th Venus is in a beautiful aspect with Pluto
and, because of this, your friends and acquaintances
are certainly in high spirits so they will be vying for
your company over the next few weeks or so. You
are positively spoiled for choice and this is creating
a nice warm glow within. What a nice position to find
yourself in.

SATURDAY 21st The most important thing about
your chart today is that the stars will allow you to dictate
terms and do things your way. There is likely to be a
creative or romantic opportunity too. But, because of

the somewhat passive nature of one of the aspects, it is up to you to make the most of it, which is true of life.

SUNDAY 22nd The Sun moves into your sign today and you begin a month when you are flooded with solar power, feel on top of the world, full of confidence and ready to take on any challenge that life is likely to throw at you. Push ahead with all self-interest, no matter in what area, and you are sure to find success.

MONDAY 23rd Mercury has decided to go into retrograde movement, a particular problem, just before Christmas. Hopefully, you have done all your shopping, because if you do any last-minute raids on the shops you could buy something you will regret. Travelling from place to place could also be complicated.

TUESDAY 24th The Full Moon today falls in your opposite sign of Cancer, so it looks as if somebody close to you is getting stressed or is perhaps a little depressed. Possibly this may have something to do with the festive period. Ask yourself if you are really pulling your weight, or are you sitting back and letting them get on with it. If the latter is true it is up to you to pitch in and help out.

WEDNESDAY 25th Other people are changeable and over-emotional today, but that may be ideal for Christmas day. If you are doing the entertaining, you will positively shine as a host or hostess. If you are visiting other people, you will be made to feel welcome and will be going a long way to contributing to a humorous day.

THURSDAY 26th This is a lazy day for you. You have decided you have done your share and now it is time to put your feet up and really relax. The only problem is, so has everybody else around you. Therefore, nothing is going to get done, and somebody is going to have to stir themselves at some point; it might as well be you.

FRIDAY 27th You may be tempted to make a raid upon the shops today, but if I were you I would save your money. Sales nowadays go on for simply ages, and there really isn't such a thing as a bargain anyway. On a more personal note, you want to make changes to a relationship, or perhaps speak up in your own defence, but for some reason you are hesitating – don't.

SATURDAY 28th Today it looks as if you have had more than your fair share of good ideas, but don't waste them on those who can't be trusted. The better the idea, the longer it will keep, and there is no need to let everyone know what you are thinking for the time being.

SUNDAY 29th The stars have, no doubt, shown you the way ahead and made you realize how much more can be possible, once you stop relying on other people to make your decisions for you. However, this can only happen once you stop allowing other people to do this. As certain individuals are not quite as trustworthy as you expected them to be it should make it easier to cut the ties.

MONDAY 30th The Moon in Virgo makes for an adventurous couple of days. The further you travel the more exciting and fulfilling your life will be. You may be visiting somebody in the hopes of celebrating the New Year with them, if so, you have made a wise decision. If you are staying at home, make sure you keep yourself busy as you will get bored easily.

TUESDAY 31st This is an ideal time for getting to know other people a good deal better. Even relatives you think you know inside out could surprise you when you engage them in deep conversation. On a romantic level, if going to a party you are sure to meet somebody exciting, but don't get too carried away, because the situation may need a little investigation before you decide whether or not you want to become part of this person's life. Happy New Year!

Moon Tables

The Moon and Your Moods

Our moods and, indeed, the strength of our intuition are clearly affected by the Moon. After all, you may ask yourself on occasions, why on earth does a well-balanced person such as me suddenly become bad tempered, frigid, emotional and sentimental on certain days? Well, I'm afraid it is all down to the position of the Moon. Why not try an experiment, and attempt to prove it to yourself?

Glance at the Moon table for any given week or month and then put it away. In the meantime, in your diary make notes of your moods and reactions to situations. Once this period has expired, rescue your book, turn to the Moon tables and you will notice a clear pattern of behaviour developing. You don't need an astrologer to work out for you that, during the week, or during the period whilst you were taking notes, the Moon was, for example, in Scorpio when you were feeling depressed, in Cancer, maybe, when you were feeling romantic and in Aries when you developed headaches and were bad tempered, for example.

Your own individual pattern is likely to be repeated monthly. However, do not give in or be surprised if you are unaffected when the Moon passes through certain signs. It may be, for example, that whilst it makes its way through Aries and Libra, you were neither elated nor depressed. What does this mean? Well, such a happening would merely suggest that these two signs are not particularly prominent on your own individual birth chart.

Female readers will probably like to take note of the fact that very often their menstrual cycle, if of normal length, will begin when the Moon is in the same one or two signs, each month. Why not be a devil and experiment? Give it a try. You have nothing to lose, and you may find out an awful lot about yourself.

FULL AND NEW MOONS FOR 1996

January	5th Full in ♋	20th New in ♑	
February	4th Full in ♌	18th New in ♒	
March	5th Full in ♍	19th New in ♓	
April	4th Full in ♎	17th New in ♈	
May	3rd Full in ♏	17th New in ♉	
June	1st Full in ♐	16th New in ♊	
July	1st Full in ♑	15th New in ♋	30th Full in ♒
August	14th New in ♌	28th Full in ♓	
September	12th New in ♍	27th Full in ♈	
October	12th New in ♎	26th Full in ♉	
November	11th New in ♏	25th Full in ♊	
December	10th New in ♐	24th Full in ♋	

KEY

♈ Aries	♌ Leo	♐ Sagittarius
♉ Taurus	♍ Virgo	♑ Capricorn
♊ Gemini	♎ Libra	♒ Aquarius
♋ Cancer	♏ Scorpio	♓ Pisces

FULL AND NEW MOONS FOR 1996

Jan	Feb	Mar	Apr	May	Jun	Jul	Aug	Sep	Oct	Nov	Dec	
♉	♋	♋	♍	♎	♐	♑	♓	♈	♊	♋	♌	1
♊	♋	♌	♍	♎	♐	♑	♓	♉	♊	♌	♍	2
♊	♌	♌	♎	♏	♑	♒	♈	♉	♊	♌	♍	3
♊	♌	♍	♎	♏	♑	♒	♈	♊	♋	♌	♍	4
♋	♌	♍	♏	♐	♒	♓	♉	♊	♋	♍	♎	5
♋	♍	♍	♏	♐	♒	♓	♉	♋	♌	♍	♎	6
♌	♍	♎	♐	♑	♓	♈	♊	♋	♌	♎	♏	7
♌	♍	♎	♐	♑	♓	♈	♊	♋	♌	♎	♏	8
♌	♎	♏	♑	♒	♈	♉	♊	♌	♍	♎	♐	9
♍	♎	♏	♑	♒	♈	♉	♋	♌	♍	♏	♐	10
♍	♏	♐	♑	♓	♈	♊	♋	♍	♎	♏	♑	11
♎	♏	♐	♑	♓	♈	♉	♊	♍	♎	♐	♑	12
♎	♐	♑	♒	♈	♉	♊	♌	♍	♏	♐	♑	13
♏	♐	♑	♓	♈	♊	♋	♌	♎	♏	♑	♒	14
♏	♑	♒	♓	♉	♊	♋	♍	♎	♏	♑	♒	15
♏	♑	♒	♈	♉	♋	♌	♍	♏	♐	♒	♓	16
♐	♒	♓	♈	♉	♋	♌	♎	♏	♐	♒	♓	17
♐	♒	♓	♉	♊	♋	♌	♎	♐	♑	♓	♈	18
♑	♓	♈	♉	♊	♌	♍	♎	♐	♑	♓	♈	19
♑	♓	♈	♊	♋	♌	♍	♏	♐	♒	♈	♉	20
♒	♈	♈	♊	♋	♌	♎	♏	♑	♒	♈	♉	21
♒	♈	♉	♊	♋	♍	♎	♐	♑	♓	♈	♊	22
♓	♉	♉	♋	♌	♍	♎	♐	♒	♓	♉	♊	23
♓	♉	♊	♋	♌	♎	♏	♑	♒	♈	♉	♊	24
♈	♉	♊	♌	♍	♎	♏	♑	♓	♈	♊	♋	25
♈	♊	♊	♌	♍	♏	♐	♒	♓	♉	♊	♋	26
♉	♊	♋	♌	♍	♏	♐	♒	♈	♉	♋	♌	27
♉	♋	♋	♍	♎	♏	♑	♓	♈	♉	♋	♌	28
♊	♋	♌	♍	♎	♐	♑	♓	♉	♊	♋	♌	29
♊		♌	♎	♏	♐	♑	♈	♉	♊	♌	♍	30
♊		♌		♏		♒	♈		♋		♍	31